Hodder

INTERMEDIATE

G N V Q

Leisure & Tourism

Leisure & Tourism

JEAN VRANIC

Hodder & Stoughton

A MEMBER OF THE HODDER HEADLINE GROUP

Orders: please contact Bookpoint Ltd, 39 Milton Park, Abingdon, Oxon
OX14 4TD. Telephone: (44) 01235 827720, Fax: (44) 01235 400454.
Lines are open from 9.00–6.00, Monday to Saturday, with a 24 hour
message answering service. Email address: orders@bookpoint.co.uk

British Library Cataloguing in Publication Data
A catalogue record for this title is available from The British Library

ISBN 0 340 743 042

First published 2000
Impression number   10 9 8 7 6 5 4 3 2
Year   2005 2004 2003 2002 2001 2000

Typeset by Fakenham Photosetting Ltd, Fakenham, Norfolk.
Printed in Great Britain for Hodder & Stoughton Educational, a
division of Hodder Headline Plc, 338 Euston Road, London NW1 3BH
by J. Arrowsmith Ltd, Bristol

CONTENTS

Chapter 4: Marketing and Promotion in Leisure and Tourism 61

Chapter 5: The Provision of Customer Services in Leisure and Tourism 97

ACKNOWLEDGEMENTS

The author and publisher would like to acknowledge the following for use of text and illustrative material:

Action Plus/Christ Barry, p.19.

Action Plus/Glyn Kirk, p.78.

Action Plus/Neil Tingle, p.20.

Action Plus/Steve Bardens, p.11.

Air Miles Travel Promotions Ltd., p.80.

AKG Photo, London, P.9.

Andrew J.G. Bell/Eye Ubiquitous/Corbis, p.27.

Elm Publications, pp.24–26.

Group Travel Organiser Magazine, Landor Travel Publications, pp.28, 74, 116.

Hulton Getty, pp.7, 9.

Lacoste, p.75.

Life File/Andrew Ward, p.34.

Life File/Dave Thompson, p.97.

Life File/John Cox, p.33.

Mary Evans Picture Library, p.10.

Middleton, Victor T.C., *Marketing Travel and Tourism*, Butterworth Heinemann, pp.68, 76.

National Railway Museum/Science and Society, p.8.

ONS, pp.18, 47, 131, 132, 135, 136.

P&O European Ferries (Portsmouth) Ltd., p.54.

Popperfoto, p.6.

The Guardian, p.24.

Thomson Holidays Ltd., p.112.

Every effort has been made to trace copyright holders but this has not always been possible in all cases; any omissions brought to our attention will be corrected in future printings.

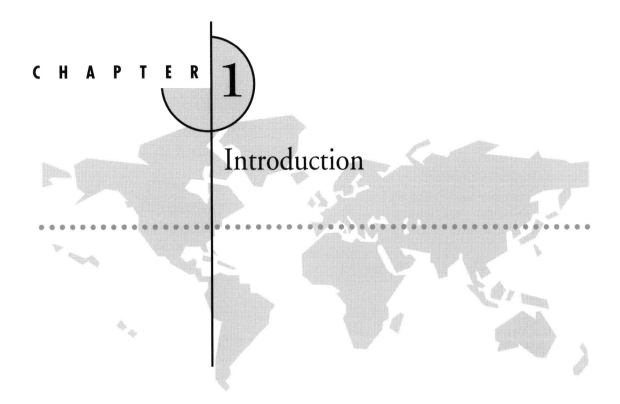

CHAPTER 1

Introduction

What is an Intermediate GNVQ?

There are two types of **unit** which you must cover for the award of a GNVQ qualification and you will study six units for the Intermediate Level:

- 3 mandatory vocational units
- 3 optional vocational units

The **mandatory vocational units** are:

- Investigating leisure and tourism
- Marketing in leisure and tourism
- Customer Service

All GNVQ Leisure and Tourism students will study these units.

The **optional vocational units** will differ depending on which awarding body's award you are taking, but they will offer a choice to follow leisure and recreation units or travel and tourism units, to help you with career progression. You may also take a mixture of both.

The key skills evidence can be gathered through the work you do for mandatory or optional units.

The following **key skills** may be evidenced through GNVQ work:

- Communication
- Application of Number
- Information Technology

There is a **unit specification** for each unit. This sets out clearly:

- the contents of the unit
- what you need to learn, and

- how you will be assessed

Most of the mandatory and option unit assessment will be done by the teaching staff in your centre and will be a continual process of gathering evidence and keeping it in a portfolio, but the marketing unit will be externally marked by the awarding body, through a set assignment or a test paper. The portfolio task for this unit could be used as preparation for the external assessment.

How do GNVQs relate to NVQs?

National Vocational Qualifications relate to performing actual jobs, whereas the GNVQ is concerned with learning about the background theory and operation of different vocations' **NVQs**. Intermediate Level GNVQ is equivalent to level 2 NVQ. In some centres it is possible to take NVQs alongside your GNVQ and this is a real help in obtaining work. For instance, you could take NVQs in Travel Services if your centre has a travel agency, you have a part-time job in an agency, or you have work experience in one.

What can I do after I gain my Intermediate GNVQ award?

On completion of the GNVQ at Intermediate level, you can progress on to other GNVQs at Advanced Level. The most appropriate path to follow would be the Vocational A Level in Leisure and Recreation or Travel and Tourism. However, you could also take another Vocational A Level such as Hospitality and Catering or Business, or go directly into employment and take relevant NVQs.

When you have finalised your studies at Intermediate Level, you will have a wider knowledge of the employment opportunities available in Leisure and Tourism and the relevant qualifications you will need to pursue your chosen career. Some suggestions are:

Academic Progression

INTERMEDIATE
LEISURE AND TOURISM

↓

ADVANCED		
LEISURE AND RECREATION	*OR*	TRAVEL AND TOURISM

↓

HND/DEGREEE		
LEISURE MANAGEMENT	*OR*	TOURISM MANAGEMENT

Progression into Employment

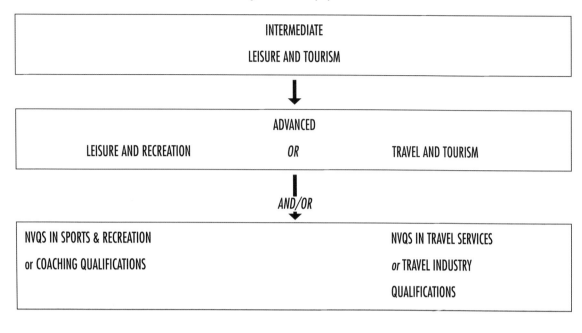

INTERMEDIATE

LEISURE AND TOURISM

ADVANCED

LEISURE AND RECREATION *OR* TRAVEL AND TOURISM

AND/OR

NVQS IN SPORTS & RECREATION

or COACHING QUALIFICATIONS

NVQS IN TRAVEL SERVICES

or TRAVEL INDUSTRY

QUALIFICATIONS

AND/OR

employment as

Sports coach

Trainee sports teacher

Theme park attendant

Travel agency sales

consultant

Resort representative

Airline cabin crew

It is important to remember that for some employment, you will be expected to work your way up to a position, however qualified you are. This is especially true of positions such as resort representatives and cabin crew, as there are minimum age limits because companies want employees with some work experience and general ability to take responsibility. They also need to be sure that an employee is independent enough to be able to work shifts and away from home.

You should be realistic in your employment expectations when you qualify at any level, and starting pay is often low. However, it can be easier to gain promotion if you have already gained a high level qualification.

You should consider carefully your chosen career path and, if necessary, adjust the way you will be able to achieve it. It is always useful to gain work experience in a relevant position alongside your studies, especially if it entails dealing with the general public as this is as essential skill in the leisure and tourism industry and will make you more attractive to a potential employer.

How to use this book

The book contains separate chapters for the different mandatory units. It provides background information on each topic, activities to help you to reinforce your understanding, and a final portfolio task which exactly meets the requirement to pass in each unit.

The Portfolio tasks are shown like this: (🗁) indicating that tasks relate to the evidence requirements of the assessment. If fully completed, the assessment evidence should be at Distinction level.

There are suggestions throughout the book for discussion points and these are indicated by a (🐾). These discussions will help you to share information and widen your knowledge of a topic.

Opportunities to include evidence for key skills are indicated by:

C   for communication

N   for application of number

IT   for information technology

Each unit can be studied independently, and you do not necessarily need to start with Unit One. However, this unit is normally selected as the starter unit for centres, and it will provide a great deal of background knowledge about the leisure and tourism industries as a base for the other units.

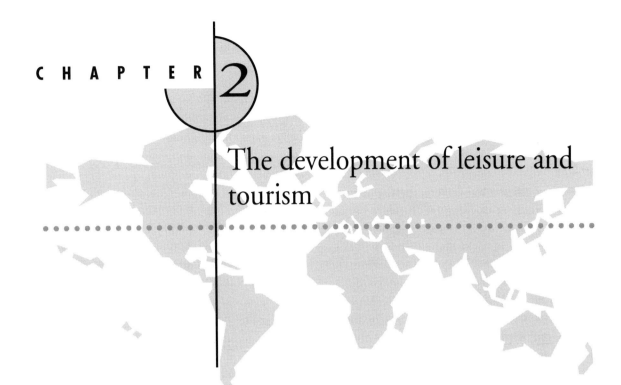

CHAPTER 2

The development of leisure and tourism

Our ancestors would have been very amused at the idea of studying 'leisure' or 'tourism' as most people in their time had very little leisure time and tourism was only for the very wealthy. Many people at the start of this century worked a six-day week for 12 hours a day. They would have Sundays off for religious reasons and to rest. There were no paid holidays. There were no labour-saving devices to help with jobs in the home, and people had large families.

Any free time was spent in simple activities – reading, walking, cycling, fishing, swimming or going to the local dance. Most of the population would also attend church regularly and be involved in activities within the church such as Scouts, a choir, the Mothers' Union.

Children had few toys, often handmade in wood, and their games were played in the streets if they lived in town. Football and rugby were played at amateur level, and in some parts of the country blood sports were still popular. Village fêtes and sports days were looked forward to eagerly.

The arrival of the travelling fair caused great excitement. Most fairs were linked to historical events related to religion, employment or trade. Many of these travelling fairs still exist today. Although there is little trading now, there are still occasionally horse fairs. The biggest horse fair in the world is held in Appleby-in-Westmoreland, Cumbria, in June and lasts a week. It has been held since 1685 and attracts thousands of 'travellers' with their caravans, who set up a huge encampment.

The Nottingham Goose Fair celebrates the

annual event when geese were driven long distances to be sold at the market, after having had their feet dipped first in tar, then sand, to provide 'shoes' for the journey. Sometimes as many as 20,000 geese would be sold at the fair. Now there is a funfair only. There are other goose fairs in the UK, as well as Crab Fairs, and Lammas Fairs.

Travelling fairs often have a regular date in different parts of the country to celebrate traditional events, such as the 'Cherry Wake' held to celebrate the finish of the cherry harvest.

Wakes or 'revels' were one of the most important events of the year for ordinary people and sometimes the only day's holiday they were allowed. Originally the feast or wake would be for some religious reason, however since the eighteenth century the religious aspect has mostly disappeared. Entertainment was the main part of the festival, and people would enjoy eating, drinking and dancing, and taking part in sports, such as sack races.

Different parts of the country became famous for their competitions such as 'gurning' (grinning) through a horse collar, when people pulled funny faces. Races were held, on foot and by horse, through the streets or through the countryside. Sometimes the runners were naked, or covered in treacle and feathers. Fancy-dress parades, maypole dancing and tugs of war were all features of these events. Wakes weeks are still held in some parts of the North of England, although nowadays the inhabitants are more likely to go to Spain for the holiday than spend it in their home town celebrating.

Male and female farm workers were hired on a yearly or half-yearly basis at 'Mop Fairs' held on May Day, Whitsun and even Christmas. People who were seeking work would wait for prospective employers to choose them. They advertised their trade by wearing or carrying emblems: a tuft of wool for a shepherd, a few strands of a mop for a maid. Farmers would agree a fee with a prospective employee and hire them. If it didn't work out, the worker could return the fee and go back to the next fair to try again. Hiring of labourers at fairs continued until the 1950s in some parts of the UK, but now the fairs are held purely for entertainment.

One of the most famous is the Mop Fair at Stratford on Avon which has been held ever 12 October since the time of Edward III. The 'Runaway Mop' was held a week later. Nowadays a modern funfair is held, with the only links to tradition being ox and pig roasts, and Morris dancing, one of our last links with traditional folk dancing in England.

Illustration of morris dancing   Source: © Popperfoto

Fairs were originally annual markets for the sale of goods, produce and animals, and the one at Newcastle is said to have been started by the Romans. One fair was supposed to run for 24 days when wool, tin, spices and wine were sold.

One of the largest fairs was on St Bartholomew's Day (24 August), held near Cambridge, with merchants travelling from all over Europe to buy and sell hops, wool and cloth, and to trade in metals and salt. Alongside the traders there were booths selling food and drink. These markets were the original 'Trade Fairs' which are now held in exhibition centres such as Olympia, G-Mex in Manchester or the NEC in Birmingham.

1937 The beach at Tower Bridge, London.
A favourite spot for East Enders in hot weather at low tide.
Source: © Hulton Getty

A reminder of these fairs is still to be found today with the old-fashioned swing-boats and hand-painted carousels, alongside the traditional games like hoopla and rifle ranges, and sideshows like the Hall of Mirrors.

The modern equivalent of these fairs are carnivals. In many parts of the world these are held on or near to Shrove Tuesday in February, but in the UK they can be held at any time of the year. Many were introduced by West Indian immigrants after the Second World War and are currently held in Birmingham, Manchester, Leeds and the biggest, London's Notting Hill Carnival, is the largest street festival in Europe. It attracts over a million people every year and is estimated to generate about £10,000,000 in trade.

The development of leisure and tourism

Tourism was popular with the richer classes, who would travel to famous seaside or inland beauty spots for different events, such as international festivals, or for their health, and young men were encouraged to travel around the world before settling down to married life.

Ordinary working people could not afford to travel abroad and until the introduction of the Holidays with Pay Act in 1938; they only had the opportunity to go away for one day at a time, usually a Sunday. Before the development of the railways, the only means of transport would be by horse-drawn carriage or steamship. Anyone fortunate to live near a large river, such as the Thames, could go on a day's excursion to the seaside resorts like Southend, where the ships would moor at the piers. Theatres and amusement arcades were

Source: National Railway Museum/Science & Society

developed at these piers for the entertainment of the day trippers. Many of these piers still exist today.

The growth of the railways in the middle of the 19th century provided ordinary people with an opportunity to see other parts of Britain, and Thomas Cook introduced the first organised evening and day visits by train.

Soon afterwards, organised visits abroad were available and the more affluent middle classes were able to visit the famous sights of Europe.

It wasn't until the introduction of cheap coach and rail holidays that the majority of people were able to go abroad. Later on, the introduction of cheap charter flights opened up the possibilities of travelling longer distances at reasonable cost.

Today, it is possible to travel almost anywhere in the world on an organised holiday at prices which are lower than they were twenty years ago.

People travelled long distances by steamships, and cruises were popular with the wealthy. Cross channel steamers and boat trips provided access to the Continent. The only means of getting a car across to the Continent was by having it lifted on and off the ferry by crane.

The introduction of transatlantic flights after the Second World War, led to a decline in the use of steamers.

Why not ask some elderly people what they did in their free time when they were young, and whether they know what their grandparents did? You will be surprised at how much the leisure and tourism industry has developed in the last 100 years.

Why do we refer to these activities as an 'industry'? This is because all the goods and services provided for leisure and tourism provide a major contribution to the economy of the country, and it has been estimated that in 2000, tourism alone will be the World's main employer.

An early coach trip in the Vatican City (1955)   *Source: © Hulton Getty*

A liner cruising the Panama Canal (1925)   *Source: © AKG Photo, London*

Imperial Airways Afternoon Tea Flight over London (1934)
Source: Mary Evans Picture Library

Tea over London

You would welcome a new and delightful experience? Then book your seat at once for an Afternoon Tea Flight over London in one of Imperial Airways' multi-engined luxury air liners! The same type as used on the Continental and Empire Services.

A dainty tea will be served to you in your comfortable armchair in the air liner while London unrolls like a map before you. Every familiar landmark is there – yet looking quite different and new from your eagle's viewpoint.

There is the familiar traffic – but crawling antwise and oddly. Here is the Tower. There is your own street! Look, Buckingham Palace! The Thames snakelike from Chelsea to its mouth. Wonderful! Fascinating beyond all describing.

Try it for the sheer pleasure of the trip and also because there is no finer way of accustoming yourself to air travel, which is so much the quickest and most comfortable means of going to the Continent and the Empire that you will use it on every possible occasion when once you have experienced the joys of flight.

Imperial Airways advertisement, 1933

Passengers in the UK

The early passengers expected and received very little in the way of comfort or amenities. On the London–Paris service, after the first few months, they were taken from city-centre to city-centre. They registered at the office of the company, or of an agent, and were then driven to the aerodrome in a hire-car. Luggage was carried to and from the aircraft by mechanics, whom it was forbidden to tip. There was a 40lb weight-limit for baggage, but it was not strictly enforced. The bait of weighing the passengers themselves was introduced during the mid 1920s.

The weighing machine at the office counter had its face politely turned inwards, so that only the clerk on duty could see it. The maximum weight allowance was for a passenger and his baggage together, so that a small, thin man would take a lot more luggage than a large, fat man. The name of one's next-of-kin was included with the facts about one's weight. The distribution of weight in the plan was almost as important as the total weight itself. If weather conditions were difficult, the airport authorities would work out the plane's centre of gravity and asks some of the passengers to move to other seats during take-off. The pilot shepherded his own passengers through the Customs on arrival and he was personally responsible for them until they and their baggage had been cleared.

Kenneth Hudson
Air Travel: A Social History

 ACTIVITY

Compare the descriptions of early air travel with today's flights. Discuss your travel experience as a group and compare them with early travellers' experiences.

Leisure and tourism is a fast developing industry, and offers many opportunities for today's young people, both for employment and for their own enjoyment.

Whilst working through the units for this qualification, you will have an opportunity of investigating the fascinating and ever changing leisure and tourism industry and identifying the type of work you would like when you complete your studies.

3

Investigating leisure and tourism

© *Action-Plus/Steve Bardens*

The importance of leisure and tourism

The leisure and tourism industry is a major source of employment worldwide and contributes a major part of the financial income of this country. Whilst investigating this industry, you will discover the wide range of services used by leisure and tourism customers and the many opportunities for working in the industry both in the UK and abroad.

There are many links between the leisure and tourism industries. For instance, whether pursuing leisure activities or travelling on business, customers will require catering facilities and entertainment. Many services, such as transport, are shared across both industries. Broadly speaking, **leisure** activities are classed as:

- sport and physical recreation
- arts and entertainment
- countryside recreation
- home-based leisure
- children's play activities
- visitor attractions
- catering

tourism includes:

- travel agents
- tour operators
- tourist information and guiding services
- accommodation and catering
- attractions
- transportation

These activities are called the 'components' of leisure and tourism.

Sectors involved in the provision of leisure and tourism facilities and activities

You will discover that leisure and tourism organisations cross over the public, private and voluntary sectors.

Public sector

The Department for Culture, Media and Sport is responsible for government policy on:

- Arts
- Broadcasting
- Cultural Objects
- Film, Music and the Press

- Government Art Collections
- Buildings, Monuments and Sites
- Libraries
- Museums and Galleries
- The National Lottery
- Sport and Recreation
- Tourism
- Media and Information Services

on a local, regional and international basis. It also has responsibilities regarding Royal Parks and Estates.

The aim of the Department is 'to improve the quality of life for all through cultural and sporting activities, and to strengthen the creative industries.'

The money raised through taxes by central government also provides grants to support specific leisure and tourism enterprises, funds UK Sport (formerly known as the UK Sports Council) and Sport England (formerly known as the English Sports Council), the National Playing Fields Association, the Arts Council, English Heritage and Tourist Boards and local councils (see Appendix 4).

You will notice that most of the responsibility is for England, Scotland, Wales and Northern Ireland have their own departments to handle many of these aspects of the industry.

If you live in these areas you will need to find out from the Scottish and Welsh Offices and the Department for Economic Development (Northern Ireland) how they manage leisure and tourism.

Private sector

This includes all organisations that operate to make a profit. This is not always easy to identify, as some facilities which were formerly in the public sector, such as leisure centres, are now operated by private organisations. Well-known companies operating in the private sector of leisure and tourism include Granada, Best Western, Rank, Virgin, Warner Holidays, and Thomson. Many of these companies operate different leisure and tourism facilities under different trading names. For example, Rank Holidays Division operates Butlin's Haven, Haven Europe, Warner and Oasis holiday centres.

THE TUSSAUDS GROUP

The Tussauds Group is one of Europe's largest operators and developers of visitor attractions with over ten million guests a year. In 1998, the Group was acquired by Charterhouse Development Capital after 20 years of ownership by Pearson plc. Charterhouse is a leading private equity firm that specialises in backing experienced management teams in quality companies with growth potential. The Tussauds Group's strategy is to develop an international entertainment business of successful visitor attractions that are special, imaginative and exceptional visitor value.

The Tussauds Group's attractions include:

- **London** – Madame Tussaud's, The London Planetarium, Madame Tussaud's Rock Circus, British Airways London Eye.
- **England** – Chessington World of Adventures (Surrey), Warwick Castle (Warwickshire), Alton Towers (Staffordshire), Thorpe Park (Surrey).
- **Europe** – Madame Tussaud's, Amsterdam.
- **Australia** – Madame Tussaud's Touring Exhibition.
- **USA** – Madame Tussaud's, Las Vegas and New York.

You will see that this group operates many different types of leisure attractions. The latest addition to the Group is the British Airways London Eye, opened for the Millennium celebrations.

 **ACTIVITY**

Identify any privately owned leisure or tourism facilities available in your area. List all the activities there. **C**

Voluntary sector

This sector includes organisations such as church youth clubs, amateur sports teams, St. John's Ambulance Brigade, playgroups, the Youth Hostels Association (YHA) and the National Trust. These organisations are funded through member subscriptions, entrance fees and some grants, including those from the National Lottery. They also receive public donations.

CASE STUDY: THE NATIONAL TRUST

On 12 January 1895, the National Trust for Places of Historic Interest or Natural Beauty was founded at Grosvenor House in London. Three moving spirits had worked determinedly towards this event: Octavia Hill, Robert Hunter and Hardwicke Rawnsley.

Each brought a different strength. Octavia Hill, famous for her housing improvement schemes, wanted 'open-air sitting-rooms' for the urban poor. Sir Robert Hunter, a skilful lawyer, had fought to preserve common land from development. Hardwicke Rawnsley, vicar of St Margaret's at Wray in Windermere, was devoted to the preservation of the Lake District for posterity. Over the succeeding one hundred years the National Trust has built on those beginnings to become the country's leading conservation charity. In 1808 Octavia Hill wrote 'we have got our first property and I wonder whether it will be our last'. That first property was Dinas Oleu, a tiny area of clifftop just above Barmouth on the Cardiganshire coast of Wales. It would have been beyond her wildest dreams to discover that by 1995 the National Trust had become such a significant landowner in England, Wales and Northern Ireland, looking after some 590,000 acres of countryside, 547 miles of coast, 207 historic houses, 162 fine gardens and much else besides (see map on page 15)

However the greatest success story this century has been the rapid increase in membership and interest in the National Trust. Over two million people are now members, including an increasing number from overseas.

ACTIVITY

Carry out a survey with your group and others of the same age group to find out which voluntary organisations they belong to or use. Which are the most popular?

Ⓒ Ⓝ ⒤⒯

ACTIVITY

Discuss with your group the types of leisure activities which you enjoy. Identify whether they take place in public, private or voluntary premises and who is responsible for the organisation of the activities. Prepare a chart showing all these activities. Ⓒ

Public sector	Private sector	Voluntary sector
Leisure centres, playing fields	Theatres and cinemas	Scouts and guides
Libraries and museums	Theme Parks	National Trust
Parks and gardens	Airports	Conservation Groups
Swimming pools	Transport companies	Special interest groups
Marinas	Hotels, guest houses	Playgroups
Play schemes	Camping and caravan sites	Sports teams
Museums	Restaurants, pubs	Red Cross
Art galleries	Nightclubs, discos	Youth hostels
Youth clubs		
Country parks		
Information centres		

TABLE 1 *The sectors responsible for leisure and tourism*

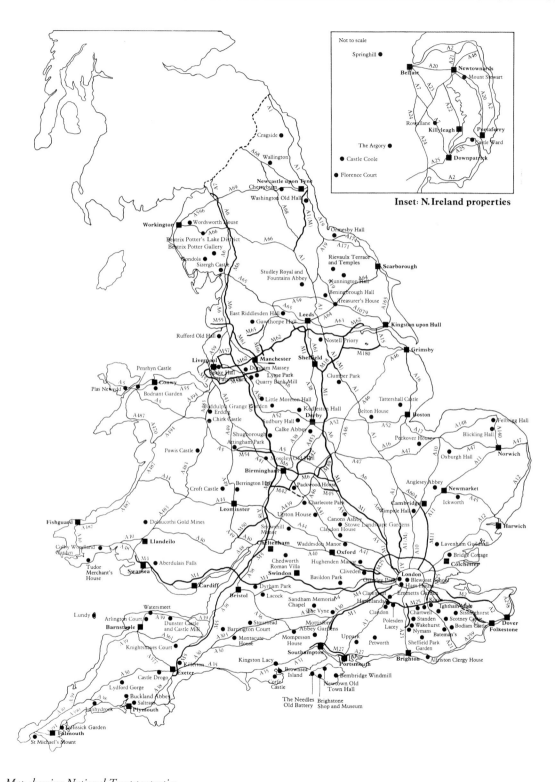

Map showing National Trust properties

To summarise then, the public sector generally means local or central government, the private sector is comprised of the organisations that operate to make a profit, and the voluntary sector is usually non-profit-making. Some examples are listed in Table 1 on page 14.

Some activities may be shared across two or three sectors. For example, a children's playgroup (voluntary) could be held in a community centre owned by the local authority (public), a private house (private) or a church (voluntary).

Increased leisure time and the availability of an increasing number of leisure facilities now offer a wide choice of activities to the public. These activities are monitored by means of a regular survey carried out by the Henley Centre. The results of the survey for 1997 to 1998 are shown in the table below.

GREAT BRITAIN						PERCENTAGES
	16–24	25–34	35–44	45–59	60 AND OVER	ALL AGED 16 AND OVER
Visit a public house	82	85	81	74	55	74
Meal in a restaurant (not fast food)	63	69	65	75	70	69
Meal in a fast food restaurant	77	74	55	34	11	48
Library	41	38	43	37	43	40
Cinema	65	51	31	23	11	34
Historic building	24	30	35	39	30	32
Short break holiday	39	35	27	26	30	31
Disco or night club	68	47	20	9	3	27
Spectator sports event	31	34	36	22	11	26
Museum or art gallery	21	18	27	26	19	22
Fun fair	27	29	23	16	6	19
Theatre	14	18	15	18	17	17
Theme park	29	22	23	10	5	17
Camping or caravanning	17	11	15	13	6	12
Bingo	11	6	7	11	16	11
Visit a betting shop	9	10	7	11	8	9

[1] In the three months prior to interview.

TABLE 2   *Participation in selected leisure activities away from home: by age, 1997–98*

Source: Leisure Tracking Survey, The Henley Centre

ACTIVITY

1. **Find the most recent survey available on leisure activities and compare the results with the survey for 1997 to 1998 in Table 2. Are there any changes? If so, can you explain why? Discuss this with a partner and summarise your conclusions.**

2. **Carry out a survey amongst the over 60 year olds in your area and compare your findings with the above. Are there any differences in the popularity of activities? What is the most popular activity amongst the over 60 year olds in your area? Discuss your findings regarding the provision of facilities for this age group.**

The components of the leisure industry

We will now examine in more detail the separate components of the leisure industry and the activities associated with each component.

Sport and physical recreation

Sport can be formally organised such as a league football match, or an informal match, such as a game with friends on the local recreation ground. Indoor and outdoor sports and physical recreation are popular leisure activities for all age groups in this country. An average of 64% of the adult population participate in at least one sporting and physical recreation activity in any four week period, according to the General Household Survey

of 1996, with walking being the most popular activity (see Table 3, page 18).

Sports and recreation facilities in most areas are mainly provided by local authorities as a result of the Town and Country Planning Act of 1947, which enabled local authorities to designate land for recreational purposes. Later Acts extended both the powers and the duties of local authorities to provide these facilities. Councils have to report on the provision of these facilities in their Annual Reports.

ACTIVITY

Identify the sports and recreation facilities in your area and mark them on a map. You should also include parks and playgrounds, and water recreation areas.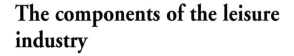

ACTIVITY

Identify one particular sports facility operated by the council, for instance a swimming pool, and find out how much the council have to contribute to operate it each year. Does it make a profit or loss? Discuss with your group whether you consider the facility to be providing good value for money to the local community.

Facilities can also be operated by voluntary organisations – for instance, small football, cricket and rugby clubs usually have their own clubhouse and pitch. They get their funds by taking subscriptions from their members, taking money in a bar, charging

GREAT BRITAIN   **PERCENTAGES**

	MALES			FEMALES		
	1987	**1990–91**	**1996–97**	**1987**	**1990–91**	**1996–97**
Walking	41	44	49	35	38	41
Snooker/pool/billiards	27	24	20	5	5	4
Cycling	10	12	15	7	7	8
Swimming		14	13		15	17
Darts	14	11		4	4	
Soccer	10	10	10			
Golf	7	9	8	1	2	2
Weightlifting/training	7	8		2	2	–
Running	8	8	7	3	2	2
Keep fit/yoga	5	6	7	12	16	17
Tenpin bowls/skittles	2	5	4	1	3	3
Badminton	4	4	3	3	3	2
At least one activity[2]	70	73	71	52	57	58

[1] Percentage aged 16 and over participating in each activity in the four weeks before interview.
[2] Includes activities not separately listed.

TABLE 3 *Participation[1] in the most popular sports, games and physical activities: by gender*

Source: General Household Survey, Office for National Statistics

admission, holding fund raising events etc. Nowadays this is often subsidised by sponsorship. Small clubs are likely to get sponsored by local companies. For instance a factory may sponsor the local boys' football team by providing their shirts (showing the sponsor's logo) every season, or provide transport to away matches.

Larger rugby clubs which used to operate on a voluntary basis are now turning professional and forming limited companies.

Large professional clubs obtain funding from a variety of sources:

- Sponsorship deals with companies such as sportswear manufacturers
- Selling merchandise to fans – replica kits, souvenir items

World student games football   *Source: © Action-Plus/Chris Barry*

- Gate receipts
- Television broadcasting rights
- Selling players
- Providing corporate hospitality (hiring out the building for conferences etc. It is even possible to get married at some famous football clubs!)

Manchester United is the richest football club in Europe, mainly due to its off pitch activities such as merchandising souvenirs, and the fact that it has fans worldwide. It has recently joined with Quality hotels to open a hotel near to the Old Trafford Ground. The next richest club is Barcelona, and their main source of income is gate receipts.

Quality kicks off in Manchester

Manchester United fans looking for a bed for the night after an evening game will not have to walk far following the opening of a new three-star hotel next to the football ground.

The 111-room Quality Hotel Manchester, which is 25 per cent owned by the football club, is the only mid-market hotel in that area of the city which is destined to become a popular area for both business and leisure.

Opposite Salford Quays and within a short distance of the UK's largest shopping mall — the Trafford Centre — the hotel is billing itself "the official hotel of Manchester United".

There are 32 executive rooms.

Public facilities include a 120-seat brasserie-style restaurant operated by a company run by celebrity chef Gary Rhodes. There are meeting facilities for up to 100 people seated theatre-style.

Weekend breaks are available from £30 per person per night.

Guests qualify for discounts at nearby attractions including Granada Studios and the Manchester United Museum.

Source: Travel News

Hospitality at Royal Ascot   *Source: © Action-Plus/Neil Tingle*

 ## ACTIVITY

1. **Consider the article from *Travel News* on page 19 and identify the links with other organisations in the area. Why was the Quality Hotel considered important for leisure and business tourism? Discuss it with a partner and list all the potential benefits from these links.**

2. **Discuss with your group all the articles that are sold with the colours and logos of football and other sports teams. Have you bought any? How much money did you spend on them?**

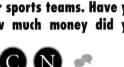

Some of Manchester United's merchandise
Source: Great Universal Catalogue

Physical education is a compulsory part of the National Curriculum, and the government has appointed a Youth Sports Unit to promote the importance of PE and sport for young people and with the responsibility of children's play. The UK Sports Institute provides support services through a network of ten regional centres of excellence. These are:

- Bath University
- Bedford
- Bisham Abbey
- Crystal Palace
- Gateshead
- Holme Pierpont/Loughborough

- Lilleshall
- Manchester
- Southampton University
- Sheffield

The government's intention is that these centres will provide the best sporting facilities and services for our leading sportsmen and women, to enable them to compete against the world's best athletes.

Additional support for promoting sport for the young has been provided through its 'World Class Programme', which provides grants to assist governing bodies in the identification of talent and development of coaching programmes, the provision of support staff, and subsistence for disadvantaged young people engaging in sports activities. The funding has already had a positive effect on the results achieved in Rowing, Swimming and Athletics Championships and the Commonwealth Games.

Income from the National Lottery has been the main source for much of this additional funding, with further funds being obtained through Pool Betting Duty.

ACTIVITY

Investigate the sports programmes on offer in your area. Are any of these being funded through the Lottery?

RECREATION FACILITIES

Recreation facilities include parks and playgrounds, sports centres bowling greens, tennis courts, cycle paths and watersports facilities. Most of these facilities will be provided by the

Map of National Parks

local authority, close to residential areas, but some receive funds from central government, through the Countryside Commission for example, who will provide grants for picnic sites, planting trees, creating footpaths. Some facilities are national, for example the National Parks which have been designated because of their natural beauty.

The Countryside Commission receives a grant from the government and is responsible for:

- the designation of national parks, areas of outstanding natural beauty and long distance footpaths and bridleways.
- providing grants for country parks, picnic sites and other countryside facilities and services including planting trees and creating footpaths.
- undertaking research into all areas of countryside management and producing educational and informative literature.

The Countryside Commission has been co-ordinating and supervising the Millenium Green project which has provided green areas for small communitities throughout England by the provision of grants.

Many areas popular for recreation depend on their natural features, such as lakes and mountains, coast, reservoirs. Some particularly beautiful parts have been bought by the National Trust, a charity, in order to keep it safe for future generations.

The National Trust owns or manages a wide variety of different properties and land throughout the UK. The Trust is funded by subscriptions from members and from donations and legacies.

Picnic areas and playgrounds are also provided near to tourist attractions such as castles, to encourage more visitors and extend their visit and all facilities have souvenir shops to boost their income.

Arts and entertainment

This includes theatres, cinema, art galleries, museums, art centres, entertainment venues, discos, dance and music classes, amusement arcades, theme parks, craft classes and centres.

Most large cities have a theatre and cinemas. Amateur drama and music groups exist throughout the country and they put on productions for the general public usually at lower cost than professional theatres can. There are touring theatre groups, some of which specialise in introducing drama to school children. Many famous professional actors and musicians started in amateur productions.

A survey carried out in 1996–1997 revealed that one in four adults in Britain said they attended plays, but fewer than one in ten went to the ballet or opera. Attendance at cultural events has changed very little in the last decade, apart from cinema attendance which rose to 124 million in 1997, mainly due to the introduction of the multiple screen cinema complexes.

Many cinemas are now sited outside city areas as part of 'leisure complexes', usually with good access from motorways and with a large population in the catchment area. Typically they will include fast-food outlets and fun pubs as well as the cinemas which have multi screens. Cinema attendance has increased greatly since these developments, but unfortunately this has led to the closure of smaller single screen cinemas in small towns.

ACTIVITY

Arrange a visit to a nearby arts centre, theatre or cinema and list all the facilities and services included. In particular look out for links with other components in leisure and tourism, for example, transport, catering or merchandising.

There are many arts and entertainment activities arranged in local communities, either by the local authority or voluntary groups. The activities are wide-ranging and can offer the opportunity to participate in everything from aerobics to the study of zoology. Classes are held in schools, colleges, community centres and church halls.

ACTIVITY

Find out what classes are held in your local community centre. For instance, where could you go to learn the latest dance craze? Who organises the classes?

MUSEUMS

We are extremely fortunate in the UK with the wide range of museums we can visit. Entrance to local art galleries and museums is usually free as they are funded by the local councils. Some of the larger National Museums have had to introduce charges to cover their costs, but recently they have received additional funding from the proceeds of the National Lottery.

Our most famous National Museums are found in London, including the National Maritime Museum, the Imperial War Museum, the Science and Natural History Museums.

Not all lottery funded projects have been successful. An attempt to spread the availability of museums all over the UK has resulted in some failures (see *Guardian* article on page 24).

Privately-owned heritage museums have been developed following different themes, e.g. the Museum of Packaging and Advertising, in Gloucester. This was originally a private collection belonging to Robert Opie and is now part of a redevelopment of the old dock warehouses at Gloucester which also includes a large Antiques Centre and the National Waterways Museum.

Advert for Beamish – Britain's favourite open air museum
Source: Group Leisure

Our industrial heritage is preserved in museums such as the Black Country Museum in Dudley, Wedgwood Visitor Centre in Stoke on Trent, Motor Museums, Mining Museums and the Beamish Open Air Museum in Durham.

In twenty-first century Britain there will be no excuses for being bored and uninspired. A welter of new visitor attractions and cultural amenities will enable people in the provinces to be more amazed, amused and educated on their doorsteps, and less dependent on traipsing to London for cultural fixes.

Soon you will be able to sample classical music in a £60 million complex in Gateshead, enjoy a simulated journey into space in Leicester, discover the secrets of the Earth's formation in Doncaster and learn about the steel industry in Rotherham.

That is the idea behind the cultural renaissance funded by billions of pounds of National Lottery money. But today it appears to be crumbling. This Tuesday creditors of the National Centre for Popular Music in Sheffield, who are owed £1m, will decide whether to accept a 10p in the pound debt settlement. If they reject it, the attraction, which opened just seven months ago funded by £11 million of Arts Council lottery cash, faces closure. Sheffield's popular music centre is just one of an uncomfortably large number of high-profile lavishly financed cultural projects currently in big trouble.

Projects funded with £300m of public money in Salford,

Rotherham, Doncaster, Leicester, York, Portsmouth and Sunderland all have question marks over their future. Those involved in the arts are beginning to raise the spectre of cultural white elephants littering the country.

The problems, they say, are manifold. Legislation framed under the last Government demanded that lottery funding had to be matched by other means. But philanthropic benefactors are only likely to donate to high-profile London projects such as the Royal Opera House, while the private sector prefers to sponsor tangible events rather than buildings.

The result is an unseemly desperation for finance to finish projects at a time when the nation is awash with lottery cash. What is more, the lottery bodies – in most cultural cases the Millennium Commission and the Arts Council – cannot originate schemes. Instead, art administrators have to convince various boards that projects are necessary and viable. This has led to wildly over-optimistic visitor projections. And when expectations are not met, income streams dwindle.

Source: The Guardian, *31 October 1999*

 # CASE STUDY

The history of transport has been one of constant change, usually in response to new technology. During the Industrial Revolution of the late 18th century a network of canals was built to facilitate the movement of goods being manufactured in the new factories at a time when journeys by road could still be long and uncomfortable. Then as the 19th century progressed the canals gradually fell into neglect as railways tracks were laid, providing even quicker and easier transportation. In the 20th century it was the turn of the railways to feel the pinch as more and more people acquired their own cars and the growth of the motorway network meant that many goods could be transported more quickly and efficiently by road.

However, in the late 20th century tourism gave a new lease of life to some transport systems that might otherwise have outlived their usefulness.

The railways

Most railway tracks in the UK were laid in three bursts of 'railway mania', in the 1830s, 1840s and 1850s. The first railways were distinguished by complex tunnels and earthworks to deal with differing gradients, and by grandiose station buildings, typified by the mid-Victorian Gothic fantasy of St. Pancras, the Elizabethan Revival-style of Brunel's Old Station in Bristol and the Classical style of Huddersfield Station. As the century pro-

gressed, however, more powerful steam locomotives could handle steeper gradients, so the
routes became simpler. Financial constraints
also led to more modest designs for stations.

By 1870 the majority of the rail network had
been laid and Britain had more than 11,000
miles of track. A few branch lines continued
to be built and when the railways were
nationalised in 1948 there were 19,600 miles
of track together with 8,294 stations. Since
then many railway lines have been axed, particularly as a result of the Beeching Report in
1963, so that only about 10,500 miles remain,
together with 2,600 stations. Railways that
had served old quarries and other industrial
sties were particularly likely to be closed as
uneconomic. British Rail inherited more than
20,000 steam engines from the private railway
companies in 1948, but by 1968 they had all
been taken out of service.

Fortunately train enthusiasts were quick to
spot the touristic potential of railways that
British Rail decided to abandon, particularly

when they ran through beautiful countryside.
So in 1951 the Talyllyn Railway Preservation
Society was created to save a narrow gauge
slate quarry railway running through spectacular scenery at Talyllyn in West Wales.
This was the world's first successful railway
preservation society and was quickly followed
by others, some of them, like the Bluebell
Railway Preservation Society in East Sussex,
run as commercial operations. Preserved railways play a particularly important part in
Welsh tourism.

The railway preservation societies usually had
two aims: to restore old steam locomotives
and operate them again, and to revitalise old
tracks in attractive countryside for the benefit
of railway buffs and tourists.

Most preservation societies are run with volunteers or with skeleton staff. Occasionally
outside help has been available. The
Peterborough Development Corporation
helped with the restoration of the Nene
Valley Railway as part of its plan to create a

The Preserved Railways of Wales

Source: Wales Tourist Board

recreation park for an expanding new town in the Nene Valley. The Manpower Services Commission also gave a £95,000 grant to help with the extension of the Kent and East Sussex Railway. The Association of Railway Preservation Societies offers advice on technical, legal and administrative problems and liaises with the British Tourist Authority, British Rail and other interested bodies for publicity purposes.

Some of the railways that have been restored used to be part of the passenger network, while others served industrial outlets. In some cases new track has been laid to carry restored steam trains, as in the grounds of Bicton House and Bressingham Hall. Stations have sometimes been restored in situ. Elsewhere fittings have been salvaged from other stations and reused. The Midland Railway Trust even moved Whitwell Station in its entirety to Butterley.

Some of the restored locomotives were acquired with the tracks from British Rail, some were brought from industrial concerns like the National Coal Board, and others were brought back from overseas. Many came from Woodham's Scrapyard in Barry which had become a graveyard for old engines in the

1960s. In the 1970s a few reproductions of famous locomotives were also built: a copy of Locomotion Number One was built in 1975 for the 150th anniversary of the Stockton-Darlington Railway, and reproductions of the trains used in the Rainhill Trails were built in 1978 for the Liverpool-Manchester Railway anniversary celebrations in 1980.

A few of the preserved railways like the Bluebell Railway operate all year round. Elsewhere services may be more limited in winter as with the Romney, Hythe and Dymchurch Railway. A few, like the Watercress Line which has a connecting station at Alton, link into the British Rail network which makes commercial passenger operation more feasible. Others operate special services like 'Santa Specials' (Nene Valley Railway) and Enthusiasts' Days when train buffs will flock in from all round the country. The Romney, Hythe and Dymchurch Railway, 'the world's smallest public railway', operates open-top carriages in summer, while the Kent and East Sussex Railway, offers passengers Pullman luxury and four course dinners on Sundays.

Source: Tourist Attractions to Heritage Tourism,
Pat Yale, Elm Publications

ENTERTAINMENT CENTRES

Many of these are multi-use facilities, such as an exhibition centre which will also be used for theatre, opera and other types of entertainment. For instance, the National Indoor Arena in Birmingham's main function is for athletics. However, it is also used to stage large operatic productions, ice shows and for the filming of the 'Gladiators' television programme.

Arts centres often house cinemas, theatres, bars and restaurants, as well as meeting rooms for temporary exhibitions, arts classes, etc.

AMUSEMENT ARCADES, CIRCUSES AND FAIRGROUNDS

Long before the introduction of computer games, amusement arcades were extremely popular and were found in the usual tourist resorts such as the seaside – when they were often on the pier, or as part of a travelling fair. Nowadays many of these machines are sited inside pubs and cafés. The modern version of the amusement arcade is the Cyber Café, where customers can use computers to access the Internet.

The largest permanent fairground in the UK is at Blackpool Pleasure Beach. It is estimated that everyone in the UK will visit Blackpool at least once in their lifetime. Many seaside resorts have permanent fairgrounds. The rides are a mixture of old-fashioned hand-painted carousel rides and the latest in electronic gadgetry, and bare-knuckle rides alongside the traditional games like hoopla and rifle ranges and sideshows like the Hall of Mirrors.

Circuses have declined in popularity, as the public's taste has grown more sophisticated. Nowadays people are able to see wildlife programmes on television or visit safari parks to see wild animals whereas fifty years ago they would have been amazed to see elephants, lions and tigers.

Circuses used to have a parade when they first arrived in a town and everyone took their children to see it. As the public has got more concerned about animal rights, circuses have had to change their programmes, so that they use only humans. However, there are still some exciting high wire and trapeze acts, and everyone enjoys clowns.

ACTIVITY

Investigate the fairs and carnivals held in your area.

Find out their original purpose and when they started. Share your findings with the rest of your group. Ⓒ 💬

Blackpool Pleasure Beach
Source: © Andrew J. G. Bell; Eye Ubiquitous/Corbis

THEME PARKS

These are the modern equivalent of the fairground and originated in the USA, when Disneyland was created. They are usually based on a main theme such as 'Gulliver's Kingdom', 'American Adventure' or 'Legoland', but many are also named after the stately home around which the park has been developed: Alton Towers, Thorpe Park, and Drayton Manor are a few examples.

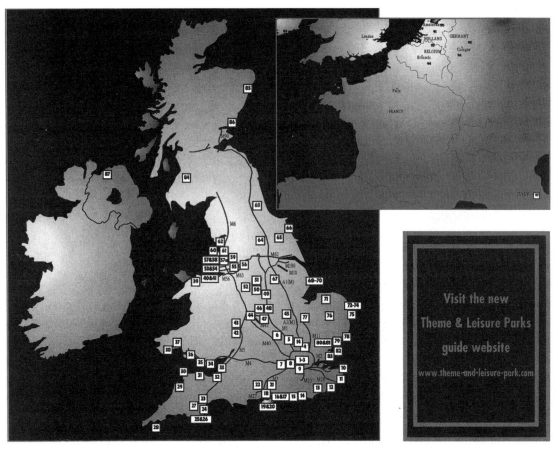

[1]	Sega World, London	[34]	Barry Island Pleasure Park
[2]	London Dungeon	[35]	Coney Beach Amusement Park
[3]	Funland & Laser Bowl, London	[36]	Mumbles Pier, Swansea
[4]	Paradise Wildlife Park, Broxbourne	[37]	Folly Farm, Begelly
[5]	Whipsnade Wild Animal Park	[38]	Oakwood, Narberth
[6]	Woburn Safari Park	[39]	Dinosaur World, Colwyn Bay
[7]	Legoland, Windsor	[40]	Knightly's Leisure Centre, Towyn
[8]	Thorpe Park	[41]	Palace Fun Centre, Rhyl
[9]	Chessington World of Adventures	[42]	Shipley's Riverside Bowl and Amusement Park,
[10]	Dreamland Fun Park, Margate		Stourport
[11]	Rotunda Amusement Park, Folkstone	[43]	West Midland Safari & Leisure Park, Bewdley
[12]	The Stade, Hastings	[44]	Cadbury World, Bournville
[13]	Drusillas Park, Alfriston	[45]	Wickstead Park
[14]	Brighton Palace Pier	[46]	Drayton Manor Park & Zoo, Tamworth
[15]	Harbour Park, Littlehampton	[47]	Dudley Zoo
[16]	New Butlin's Family Entertainment Resort,	[48]	Twycross Zoo, Atherstone
	Bognor Regis	[49]	American Adventure World, Ilkeston
[17]	Funland, Hayling Island	[50]	Heights of Abraham
[18]	Clarence Pier Amusement Park, Southsea	[51]	Gulliver's Kingdom, Matlock Bath
[19]	Sandown Pier	[52]	Alton Towers
[20]	Isle of Wight Zoo	[53]	New Palace Adventureland & Speed Karting
[21]	Marwell Zoological Park		Circuit, New Brighton
[22]	Paultons Park, Near Romsey	[54]	The Beatles Story
[23]	Crealy Park, Exeter	[55]	Gulliver's World, Warrington
[24]	Grand Pier, Teignmouth	[56]	Granada Studios Tour, Manchester
[25]	Paignton Pier	[57]	Pleasureland Amusement Park, Southport
[26]	Woodlands Leisure Park, Dartmouth	[57a]	Southport Zoo
[27]	Trago Mills, Stover	[58]	St Annes Pleasure Island
[28]	Flambards Village Theme Park, Helston	[59]	Camelot Theme Park, Chorley
[29]	Milky Way Adventure Park, Clovelly	[60]	Blackpool Pleasure Beach
[30]	Watermouth Castle, Ilfracombe	[61]	Children's Corner, Cleveleys
[31]	New Butin's Family Entertainment Resort,	[62]	Frontierland, Morecambe
	Minehead	[63]	The New MetroLand, Gateshead
[32]	Brean Leisure Park, Burnham On Sea	[64]	Lightwater Valley Theme Park, Ripon
[33]	Grand Pier, Weston-super-Mare	[65]	Flamingo Land Theme Park & Zoo, Malton

[66]	Carousel Park, Bridlington
[67]	Sundown Adventureland, Retford
[68]	The Magical World of Fantasy Island,
	Ingoldmells
[69]	Botton's Pleasure Beach, Skegness
[70]	New Butlin's Family Entertainment Resort,
	Skegness
[71]	The Thursford Collection, Fakenham
[72]	Joyland, Great Yarmouth
[73]	Great Yarmouth Pleasure Beach
[74]	Britannia Pier, G. Yarmouth
[75]	Pleasurewood Hills Theme Park, Lowestoft
[76]	Banham Zoo
[77]	Linton Zoo
[78]	Manning's Amusement Park, Felixstowe
[79]	Walton Pier
[80]	Colchester Zoo
[81]	Rollerworld, Colchester
[82]	Clacton Pier & Living Ocean Aquarium
[83]	Adventure Island, Southend
[84]	Loudoun Castle Park, Ayrshire
[85]	Aberdeen Amusement Park
[86]	Arbroath Pleasureland
[87]	Barry's Amusement Park, Portrush
[88]	Perks Pleasure Park, Co. Cork, Eire
[89]	Duinrell, Holland
[90]	Dolfinarium Harderwijk, Holland
[91]	Etieling Family Leisure Park, Holland
[92]	Mell Park, Belgium
[93]	Bobbejaanland, Belgium
[94]	Walibi, Belgium
[95]	Warner Bros Movie World
[96]	Phantasialand, Germany
[97]	Mirabilandia, Italy

Theme and leisure parks, 1999

Source: Group Travel Organiser Magazine, Landor Travel Publications

The parks combine extensive grounds with exciting rides. Many of the rides are spectactular achievements of technology and every year new rides are added which go higher/faster/are more frightening. They aim to provide a full day out for all the family.

Countryside recreation

ACTIVITY

Discuss theme parks with your group. How many of you have visited one? What was the best part of the visit? Were they any unusual features? How much did it cost? Was it value for money? C N

Many areas popular for recreation depend on their natural features such as lakes and mountains, coast and reservoirs. Some particularly beautiful parts have been bought by the National Trust in order to preserve them for future generations. Walking, mountain bike races, quad biking, rambling, ballooning, sailing and fishing are some of the main activities carried out outdoors and in the countryside. Fishing has the highest number of participants of any sport in the UK.

Improved access to areas such as the Lake District, more leisure time and more available income has increased the opportunities for people to participate in these activities.

WILDLIFE CENTRES

Wildlife centres are widely accessible. There are safari parks, zoos, water and domestic fowl centres, shire horse centres, donkey farms – the list is endless. The first safari park was opened at Longleat, and offered the public the first opportunity of seeing lions in a natural environment, not behind the bars of a

Illustration of a wildlife centre

Source: Group Leisure, *February 1999*

zoo enlosure or at a circus. Many wildlife centres which started as rescue centres for instance, the Seal Sanctuary in Cornwall, are now open to the public; this brings them valuable income.

CASE STUDY

The Forestry Commission is the government department responsible for the management of all publicly-owned forests in Britain. Its mission is to:

'Protect and expand Britain's forests and woodlands and increase their value to society and the environment.'

There are more than a million hectares of forest available for timber production, and which are available for recreation and public access. Some facts related to recreation in forest and woodland are:

- More than 70% of all adults have visited British forests in the last few years.
- Around 350 million day trips are made to forests each year.
- They are regularly used by dog walkers and holiday-makers.

Activities which take place in forests include:

- walking
- cycling
- horse riding
- orienteering
- camping
- caravanning
- fishing
- birdwatching, and many more outdoor activities

The commission also owns log cabins, which are available for holiday rentals.

Other organisations concerned with the countryside include the Countryside Commission and The Ramblers Association, which regularly campaigns to protect the natural beauty of the countryside. The Ramblers Association was responsible for preventing the privatisation of Forestry Commission land. Current campaigns are for the 'right to roam' the countryside, and the re-opening of all public footpaths.

The public are becoming more aware of the health benefits of taking part in outdoor activities, and concern for the environment has led to the introduction of many new types of holidays. One company – Country Lanes – won an award from the English Tourist Board in 1998 for its cycling holidays.

Country Lanes Wins Green Award

'Country Lanes tackles the major issue of transport and the environment with a winning combination for the 21st century.' That's how the judges described bicycle touring specialist Country Lanes, this year's winner of the English Tourist Board's coveted *England for Excellence Green Award for Tourism and Environmental Management*.

'I'm thrilled that we have been recognised for our contribution to tourism and the environment,' says Susan Achmatowicz, Country Lanes' owner. 'We actively encourage visitors to reach the country-side by rail and explore by bicycle and it's great to know that our sustainable approach to tourism is valued.'

The panel of judges was impressed with Country Lanes nation-wide programme of cycling day excursions, short breaks and longer tours, all of which begin with a rail journey. Started five years ago from an office in Fordingbridge, Hampshire, Country Lanes has expanded through a network of cycle centres providing quality equipment for hire at rail station locations including Brockenhurst in the New Forest, Moreton-in-Marsh in the Cotswolds and Windermere in the Lake District.

When asked about the significance of winning the Green Award, Susan explains: 'Winning the Green Award is fantastic news for Country Lanes, and will raise the profile of issues related to cycling, integrated transport and sustainable tourism. We're hoping that the publicity generated by the Award will help in our search for investors and sponsors to join Country Lanes' as we grow our network of cycle centres at rural rail stations.'

Rail-cycle tourism initiative on track at Brockenhurst station

The award-winning bicycle touring specialist Country Lanes has opened the nation's first cycle hire centre to operate from a restored railway carriage at Brockenhurst station in the New Forest.

The idea is the brainchild of Country Lanes owner Susan Achmatowicz. 'Forty years ago,' says Susan, 'rolling stock was built to transport *cars* by rail. We're taking obsolete Motorail units and converting them into modern cycle hire centres for rural stations with leisure cycling potential. Brockenhurst is our first installation and quite appropriately we've positioned the carriage in a Motorail bay that was taken out of commission many years ago.'

The railway carriage is proving to be an attraction in its own right. 'Railway enthusiasts are enquiring about the history of this particular carriage,' says Susan, 'so we're planning an information board with details of the carriage's provenance.' This unique leisure cycling facility respects the heritage of our railways, enhances the station environment and provides visitors to the New Forest with an integrated transport alternative to car-congested New Forest villages.

Externally the Motorail unit is in keeping with the railway environment and heritage; but inside it is fully equipped with today's modern technology – 24 speed mountain bikes for hire and an Internet connection for on-line bookings.

Source: Country Lanes, 8 Shaftesbury St, Fordingbridge SP6 1JF.

ACTIVITY

Examine the information on the Forestry Commission and Country Lanes (pages 30 and 31). How many links within leisure and tourism and public, private and voluntary sectors can you identify?

Leisure activities at home

The growth of technology has led to increased leisure-time use of computers, video recorders, and electronic musical instruments. Satellite and cable television has increased the numbers of channels available to everyone.

Gardening continues to be a popular pastime, as indicated by the growth of garden centres and attendance figures at flower shows, while visits to famous gardens continue to be popular, particularly with older people.

FLORA Garden Tours

FLORA Garden Tours run holidays based in famous old Cambridge or Oxford Colleges. You merely pay for the accommodation and, if you wish, for a choice of individual tours from a range covering the history and architecture of the city and its University buildings, the College gardens and the nearby stately homes and gardens. There are also theme tours on medieval life and buildings and famous literary figures, and famous scientists connected with the colleges.

Source: www.flora.co.uk

Craftwork has regained its popularity, in spite of the increased time spent watching television, with many people making handcrafted articles in the home for sale.

Craft fairs are held all over the country. Lists of craft fairs can be found on the Internet, giving an indication of the popularity of such events.

ACTIVITY

Carry out your own research on the Internet to find out about crafts events near to your home or in another part of Britain.

Other home-based activities include reading, board and card games, listening to music and cooking for pleasure.

ACTIVITY

List all the activities that your group carry out at home. How have these activities changed in the last ten years? Ⓒ

Children's play activities

Children's leisure time is often simply taken us 'playing'. Two generations ago, children would have played in the street, but nowadays they either have to play in their own homes and gardens or in parks and play areas. Many children's games have existed for centuries, but are dying out because they are no longer passed on from one child or another.

New housing estates are now planned to incorporate safe children's play areas, and the commercial world has realised the marketing potential of providing playrooms, playgrounds and activity organisers in shopping areas and pubs or restaurants. 'The Wacky Warehouse' is a good example of such an enterprise – children can play safely in the Warehouse whilst their parents enjoy a meal or a drink in the pub. Safeway supermarkets provide crèche facilities for shoppers, cross Channel ferries have soft play centres and some large stores, such as IKEA have children's cinemas. Playgroups are available for pre-school children and there are after-school and holiday clubs for children, where they play organised games. Play equipment manufacturers are constantly providing new ideas for imaginative play (see below).

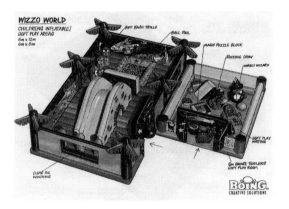

Product promoting imaginative play for children

Source: BOING Creative Solutions

Source: © Life File/John Cox

ACTIVITY

Investigate the activities of different age groups in your area and draw up a chart showing which activities are most popular with the following age groups:

**Under 16s
18–30
30–40
40–50
50–60
over 60s.**

Also show on your charts which activities are for individuals, such as fishing, which are for all ages such as line-dancing and which are for families and groups such as bowling, playing sports. Identify those which are low cost, and those which are expensive.

Visitor attractions

We are extremely fortunate in this country that we have hundreds of visitor attractions to suit every age and interest. As we cannot rely on good weather all year, tourist destinations have developed a wide variety of places to visit. As well as theme parks and museums with historical connections, it is possible to visit such attractions as the *Mary Rose* in Portsmouth – a restored vessel dating from the time of Henry VIII – the Nuclear Energy Centre at Sellafield and the Millenium Dome.

Millennium Dome

Source: © Life File/Andrew Ward

Attractions and Entertainment

At the heart of the Dome will be a central area of 72 metres in diameter, with a potential of 10,000 mixed seating and standing capacity. This will be the setting for the central experience – a show with live performers and stunning visual effects – created by Mark Fisher and Peter Gabriel. This will be repeated throughout the day. At times when the show is not playing, other more informal, live entertainment will be provided here, as well as on the Piazza Stage, and, in good weather, in Meridian Gardens.

Ranged around the central area, in entrancing and varied settings, will be 14 spectacular exhibition zones – designed by the best of British and international designers and architects – exploring the choices facing humankind in the 21st century and beyond.

Visitors will explore and interact with state-of-the-art exhibits focusing on the past, present and future of work; learning; rest; play; money; dreams; talk; body; mind; spirit; local, national and global environment. Each zone will be uniquely designed, incorporating stunning, hi-tech, interactive attractions that will educate, inspire and entertain.

Alongside the Dome is the Entertainment Zone, a theatre with an auditorium capacity of 5,000 with film and concert facilities. Situated outside the Dome, separately ticketed events will be held here.

Live entertainment and performances will take place in selected areas throughout the day both within the Dome and in the Piazza.

Visitor Numbers
- The Dome will accommodate up to 35,000 visitors per session (a session = Daytime or Evening).
- On peak days, two sessions may operate. Peak days will fall on weekends, school holidays, Bank Holidays and on weekdays during the summer holidays.

Visitor Amenities
- There will be a tourist information centre, convenience store, bureau de change, post boxes and automated banking facilities all within or adjacent to the Dome.
- Within the Dome there will be lockers for visitors' belongings – for obvious security reasons, oversized bags will not be allowed into the Dome.
- The Dome will generally feel cooler in winter and warmer in summer, i.e. visitors will experience seasonal temperatures similar to that in a shopping mall. Cloakroom facilities will be available.
- There will be the Babycare facilities in every set of toilets (male & female) in the Dome. As there will be no stroller hire, families are advised to bring their own. There will be no crèche facilities.

Shops at the Dome
In the region of 20 shops will sell a wide range of Millennium merchandise and quality souvenirs.

Catering
There will be around 30 different restaurants and cafés of all categories and an international food court. There will be no group reservations for catering other than for banqueting and corporate hospitality in restaurants.

Fun Facts
- The enclosed volume of the Dome is 2.1 million metres cubed.
- This is 3.8 billion pints.
- The equivalent of 12.8 million barrels of beer.
- This is the same volume as 1,100 Olympic sized swimming pools.
- The Dome could contain more than 18,000 double decker buses or two Wembley Stadiums or 13 Albert Halls or 10 St Paul's Cathedrals or Egypt's Pyramid of Giza or the Eiffel Tower (on its side).
- It could cover the whole of Trafalgar Square and all the surrounding buildings up to Admiralty Arch (including Nelson's Column).
- The total weight of all the air contained within the Dome will make it heavier than the Dome's structure.
- The Dome will be situated next to the largest underground station in Europe.
- The Dome will house the biggest concentration of visitor attractions under one roof in the world.
- The Dome is situated on a 181 acre site.
- It has the biggest roof in the world – covering 20 acres or 80,000 square metres.
- It is the largest Dome in the world – twice the size of the USA's Georgia Dome.
- It is the largest fabric structure in the world – one million square feet of PTFE coated Teflon.
- It is the strongest fabric building – it could support the weight of a jumbo jet.

British Airways "London Eye"

NEW FOR 2000

The worlds' largest observation wheel located opposite Embankment. Its gradual 30 minute rotation will give clients views of up to 25 miles of the city and will be the 4th largest structure in London.

BRITISH AIRWAYS
LONDON eye

The London Eye

Source: Greatdays Travel Group

Work has started on a new £4.5m Wedgwood Visitor Centre at the company's factory in Barlaston, Staffordshire. The new attraction will be called 'The Wedgwood Story' and is set to open next spring.

The initiative will see Wedgwood opening the factory to groups. Discreet barriers will enable them to visit the factory floor in total safety, and without disrupting production. A route will enable groups to see all the key processes involved in producing the fine bone china tableware, from delicate manual tasks like 'fettling' – removing seams, to 'firing' inside 100 metre long ovens.

A £1m re-fit of the existing Visitor Centre will also see the introduction of a host of extra opportunities for groups to produce their own family heirlooms of the future!

Source: Group Leisure Magazine

Many industrial buildings have been turned into visitor attractions. For example, the site of Brierley Hill steelworks is now a major shopping mall called Merry Hill. Many factories are open to the public for factory tours and to sell direct to the public. These include Dartington Crystal, Worcester Porcelain, Wedgwood China and many breweries. It is possible to go down a coal mine in Wales, visit the film sets at Granada Studios, see how chocolate is made at Cadbury's World and how the Thames Barrier works in London. The list is endless.

Visitors find out more at Royal Crown Derby.

Source: Group Leisure Magazine

ACTIVITY

Prepare a short one page guide to local heritage attractions in your area. C IT

ACTIVITY

Obtain the most recent attendance figures for one of the attractions in Table 5 (see page 36) and compare them. C N

Table 4 gives an indication of how many visitor attractions we have in the UK.

(MILLIONS)	HISTORIC HOUSES	GARDENS	MUSEUMS AND ART GALLERIES	WILDLIFE SITES	OTHER	ALL
England	58.82	12.88	63.31	19.84	165.38	320.23
N Ireland	0.60	1.10	0.94	0.48	6.20	9.33
Scotland	7.24	2.04	10.19	2.32	27.04	48.82
Wales	2.44	0.31	2.74	1.01	12.01	18.50
UK	69.10	16.33	77.18	23.66	210.63	396.89

TABLE 4 *Visits to attractions (1997)*   *Source: www.staruk*

ATTRACTION	THOUSANDS
1 Madame Tussaud's, London	2,799
2 Alton Towers, Staffordshire	2,702
3 Tower of London	2,615
4 Natural History Museum, London	1,793
5 Chessington World of Adventures, Surrey	1,750
6 Canterbury Cathedral	1,613
7 Science Museum, London	1,537
8 Legoland, Windsor	1,298
9 Edinburgh Castle	1,238
10 Blackpool Tower, Lancashire	1,200
11 Windermere Lake Cruises, Cumbria	1,132
12 Windsor Castle, Berkshire	1,130
13 Flamingo Land Theme Park, Yorkshire	1,103
14 London Zoo	1,098
15 Victoria and Albert Museum, London	1,041
16 Drayton Manor Park, Staffordshire	1,002
17 St. Paul's Cathedral, London	965
18 Kew Gardens, London	937
19 Roman Baths and Pump Room, Bath	934
20 Thorpe Park, Surrey	912

TABLE 5 *Top twenty attractions charging admission in 1997*   *Source: Social Trends*

Free attractions with attendances of two million or more in 1997 include: Albert Dock, Liverpool; Blackpool Pleasure Beach; The British Museum; Eastbourne Pier; Magical World of Fantasy Island, Lincolnshire; The National Gallery; The Palace Pier, Brighton; Pleasureland Amusement Park, Southport; Strathclyde Country Park; Sutton Park, Sutton Coldfield; Westminster Abbey; York Minster.

Catering

There is a wide range of catering available in the UK from the original fast-food outlets – fish and chip shops – to the top-class restaurants featured in guides such as *Michelin*. Every taste is catered for and the standard is generally good. Recently 'balti' meals – which are a type of curry – appeared as the favourite take-away meal, having overtaken fish and chips. Dishes from all over the world are now served in our restaurants. There are many Italian, Greek, Indian, Pakistani, Bangladeshi and Chinese restaurants in the main cities and the 'take-away' meal is a common feature.

Pubs have also extended their range of food. The introduction of all-day opening in pubs and the emphasis on family customers, has encouraged publicans to offer a wide variety of traditional and unusual dishes.

The popularity of McDonald's has also increased the number of competitors offering hamburger-type meals. Access to cheap holidays in the USA has widened interest in American cuisine, with many of the dishes copied by our pubs. American catering organisations such as McDonald's, and Dunkin Donuts are found in many city centres.

Outside catering is also a major business in the UK with mobile catering vehicles travelling from event to event, attending functions and serving snacks at the roadside. The increased use of the motorcar and development of the motorways has led to the construction of large service areas – originally refuelling stations – which now include restaurants, rest areas, cloakrooms, children's play centres, amusement arcades, shops and accommodation.

ACTIVITY

Consider your local area and draw up a short guide to eating out using different categories: British, Asian, Oriental, European, American style food. Show whether they are budget, average or expensive types of establishments. Try to obtain sample menus and compare them. Ⓒ ⒤Ⓣ Ⓝ

Facilities used for leisure

Most communities offer a wide range of leisure facilities in addition to those provided for leisure and recreation which you identified earlier. These include:

- leisure centres
- health clubs
- cinemas (single-screen or multi-screen)
- pubs and restaurants
- community centres
- clubs (Football, Tennis, Youth, Scouts, Guides, Drama, Dance, Mother and toddler, Over 60s, Gardening, Women's Institute, Photography, and many more)

- parks and gardens
- playgrounds
- school halls and playing fields
- church and village halls
- museums and libraries

ACTIVITY

Many of the above facilities are provided by the local authority and are paid for out of local council taxes.

Identify which are publicly owned, privately owned or run by a charity or voluntary organisation in your area. Ⓒ

ACTIVITY

1. **Discuss your own leisure time activities with your group.** Ⓒ

2. **Draw up a list of the most popular activities showing:**
   - **how often people are engaged in them?**
   - **how much money they spend.**

   Ⓒ Ⓝ

3. **Using graphs, draw up a report showing the average amount spent on each of these activities by each person.**

   Ⓒ Ⓝ ⒤⒯

Leisure products and services

As a service industry, it is sometimes difficult to imagine that there are 'products' (see diagram on page 40).

These products are offered across a range of leisure facilities, and the service supplied needs to be consistently high in order to maintain a business. Sports activities can range from martial arts classes to tennis.

A recent study estimated that nearly £10 billion was spent on sports related goods and services, with gambling accounting for nearly 30% of that. The introduction of the National Lottery has greatly increased that total, with a total number of tickets sold rising to as many as 83 million for one Superdraw.

Sports-related goods include: replica kits, souvenirs and other merchandise, videos, books, sportswear and equipment, boats, and magazines and videos related to sport; and represents approximately 2% of all consumer spending.

In addition to the goods purchased for direct use by consumers, the development of leisure facilities has led to a dramatic rise in the supply of all types of products to leisure organisations. Examples include:

- sauna cabins, steam rooms, solarium
- soft play equipment
- playground fittings and furniture
- seating, staging and fencing for events
- flags, banners, posters
- marquees and mobile housing units
- fitness equipment
- swimming pool products and safety aids
- security equipment

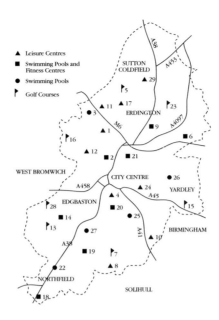

Legend (map):
- ▲ Leisure Centres
- ■ Swimming Pools and Fitness Centres
- ● Swimming Pools
- ⚑ Golf Courses

p = Planned or opening soon.

\# = Indoor provision suitable for persons with disability.

			SWIMMING										SPORTS			HEALTH & FITNESS											
			LENGTH SWIMMING	LEARNER POOL	LEISURE FUN POOL	FLUME	WAVES	WOMENS ONLY	PARENT & BABY	SWIMMING LESSONS	AQUA NATAL	DIVING POOL	BADMINTON	SQUASH	GOLF COURSE	SAUNA & STEAM	FITNESS GYM	FREE WEIGHTS	CIRCUIT TRAINING	FITNESS TESTING	AQUA AEROBICS	AEROBICS	STEP AEROBICS	SPA POOL	TONING TABLE	SUN BEDS	BEAUTY TREATMENT
1	Alexander Stadium #	356 8008														★	★					★	★			1	
2	Aston Newtown Swimming Pool	359 2370	★	★					★	★							★										
3	Beeches Swimming & Fitness Centre #	358 6296	★	★					★	★						★	★									3	
4	Birmingham Sports Centre #	440 1021											★			★	★	★	★	★		★	★				p
5	Boldmere Golf Course	354 3379													18												
6	Castle Vale Swimming Pool #	749 4644	★						★													★	★			1	
7	Cocks Moors Woods Golf Course	444 3584													18												
8	Cocks Moors Woods Leisure Centre #	441 1996			★	★	★		★	★	★		★				★		★	★	★	★	★			p	p
9	Erdington Swimming Pool	373 0520	★						★							★						★			★	3	
10	Fox Hollies Leisure Centre #	778 4112	★	★				★					★	2			★		★	★	★	★	★			1	
11	Great Barr Leisure Centre #	325 0104											★									★	★				
12	Handsworth Leisure Centre #	523 6336	★	★				★	★	★	★		★				p					★	★				
13	Harborne Golf Course	427 1204						★							9												
14	Harborne Swimming Pool	427 1174	★					★	★	★							p					★	★			2	
15	Hatchford Brook Golf Course	743 9821													18												
16	Hilltop Golf Course	554 4463													18												
17	Kingstanding Leisure Centre #	377 7890			★	★		★	★	★	★						★					p	★			8	1
18	Lickey Hills Golf Course	453 3159													18												
19	Linden Road Swimming Pool	472 4500		★					★	★																	
20	Moseley Road Swimming Pool	440 0150	★	★				★	★	★												★					
21	Nechells Swimming Pool	327 0835	★						★	★						★											
22	Northfield Swimming & Fitness Centre #	475 1058	★	★					★	★						★	★				★	★	★	★		4	★
23	Pype Hayes Golf Course	351 1014													18												
24	Small Heath Leisure Centre #	773 6131	★	★				★	★	★			★	3			★	★	★		★	★	★				
25	Sparkhill Swimming & Fitness Centre	772 1873	★	★				★	★	★						★	★				p	★	★			2	
26	Stechford Cascades #	783 5596	★	★	★	★		★	★	★							★				★	★	★			4	
27	Tiverton Road Pool & Fitness Centre	472 0020	★	★					★	★						★	★					★				2	
28	Warley Golf Course	429 2440													9												
29	Wyndley Swimming Pool	354 7743	★	★					★	★	★	★															
30	Wyndley Leisure Centre #	354 7741											★	6		★	★		p		★	★	★	★	★	2	5	★

Birmingham – a city offering a wide range of leisure activities

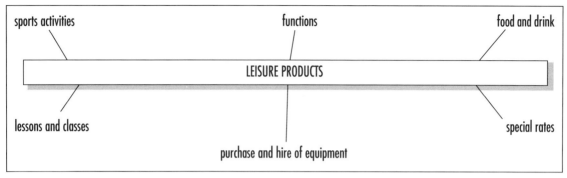

Leisure products

Using the trade press, and other directories, research items of equipment used in leisure facilities. Consider the links with all the industries involved. Ⓒ

Winter sports enthusiasts often hire equipment in a resort. It is also possible to hire watersports and camping equipment, roller skates and ice skates.

Classes are held at leisure centres, adult education centres, community centres and private training organisations for all types of sport. The most commonly held are for swimming, horseriding, football skills, tennis, martial arts and yoga, but there are many more.

Special rates are offered at these centres for off-peak use, families, the unemployed, season tickets, children and senior citizens. Members of groups often obtain discounts. Some local authorities have introduced 'Leisure Passports' for residents, which offer discounts on a wide range of leisure facilities, including local theatres and leisure centres. Many hotels now have fitness centres open to non-residents, who join as club members.

The types of functions held vary from car boot sales to garden fêtes, dog shows, carnivals, music festivals, and exhibitions and shows. A typical exhibition centre may be used for:

- collectors fairs
- dog shows
- leisure exhibitions
- flower shows
- product launches
- wedding exhibitions
- career festivals
- pop concerts

The NEC in Birmingham is the venue for the Crufts Dog Show, The Clothes Show and the Good Food Show, drawing visitors from all over the country and abroad.

Many smaller functions, in contrast, may simply be held in a field or on a sports ground.

1. Visit your local leisure centre and find out what 'products' it offers.

2. Find out whether you have any suppliers

of equipment for the leisure industry in your area.

3. **Investigate the different uses made of leisure facilities in an area. For example, a sports hall being used for other events.**

Travel and tourism

Travel and tourism includes:

- All forms of transport and the booking agents for them;
- Transport facilities such as airports, ferry ports, railways;
- Accommodation from camping and caravan parks to 5-star hotels;
- Visits within the UK and abroad for day trips, short breaks or longer holidays;
- Tour operation and travel agents;
- Tourist attractions such as heritage sites, theme parks;
- Tourism information services;
- Inclusive or 'package' tours and holidays;
- Incoming, outgoing and domestic tourism.

Many of the activities classed as travel and tourism are dependent on the leisure and recreation industry for part of the activity. For instance, tourists visit sites of historic importance, theme parks and theatres. They use catering and accommodation services and transportation.

All these activities are made possible by different organisations providing accommodation, hospitality and catering, making travel arrangements or co-ordinating the provision of services for tourists. Some of these arrangements are made by privately-owned organisations – for example, travel agents – others by local authorities who are responsible for parks,

libraries, museums, information centres, sports and leisure centres as discussed earlier.

Tourism

You need to understand what tourism means. The general definition is that travellers are classed as tourists if:

- they are travelling away from their usual place of work or home
- they intend to return

Further distinctions are made between those tourists who stay away overnight and those who only visit for a day.

The main reasons for tourism are:

- holidays
- business
- visiting friends and relations (VFR)

Other visitors to an area, for instance for study purposes, or to seek medical treatment, or to attend a sports event, will also use facilities provided for tourists.

What is the tourism industry?

In England, it's an industry with 120,000 businesses – that's eight times the number of businesses in the clothing industry – and provides jobs for about 1.5 million people. These businesses – from the ice cream salesman, to the Tourist Information Centre, to the multi-national hotel chains – provide accommodation, entertainment and information to tourists from England and from overseas. Tourism is of huge economic and social value to England. It brings new jobs to areas hit by the decline of other industries and provides a boost to our quality of life. On average, for each £30,000 spent in tourism, one job is created. Tourism accounts for 6% of England's GDP and 10% of consumer spending.

Source: English Tourism Council (formerly English Tourist Board) 1998

⬛	15 and over
⬛	10–14
⬛	5–9
⬜	4 and under

Domestic holidays[1] taken by Great Britain residents: by destination, 1996

Source: British National Travel Survey, British Tourist Authority

INCOMING AND DOMESTIC TOURISM

Britain earned about £12 billion from incoming tourism in 1997 and 25.5 million visitors came here. The British Tourist Authority has estimated that 'by 2003, overseas visitors will spend £18 billion a year in the UK, 47% more than in 1997'. The UK was fifth in the world in terms of visitor numbers, in 1997.

As shown in Table 6, tourism to the UK (incoming) is a major source of income and employment, and is one of its most important industries and an 'invisible export', i.e. money spent by foreign visitors means they are bringing in their currency from abroad. The money spent by our own residents on tourism is also a very important part of the economy.

Millions	Trips	Nights	Spending
UK residents	133.6	474	£15,075
Overseas visitors	25.5	223	£12,244
Total	**159.1**	**697**	**£27,319**

TABLE 6 *Volume and spending of tourists in the UK (1997)*
Source: www.staruk

Some facts on domestic tourism (1997):

● In 1997 the British took 30 million seaside holidays (more than 4 nights) in the UK.

● They spent £4.7 billion.

● 110 million day trips to the seaside were taken in 1996.

● 22% of all long holidays were taken in the West Country.

● Self-catering is the most popular type of accommodation.

● 38% of holidays in Britain are taken in July and August.

● Almost half of all holidays taken in Britain were spent at the seaside.

As Britain is made up of islands, it is hardly surprising that our coastline is a major attraction. The five coastal National Parks and 26 coastal Areas of Outstanding Natural Beauty in England, Wales and Northern Ireland are an indication of the rich varied coastline that we can offer visitors. Most UK residents can reach part of the coastline within a few hours of home, and a visit to the seaside is particularly popular at weekends and on Bank Holidays.

ACTIVITY

Examine the map (shown on page 42) and discuss which areas are the most popular with UK tourists. What are the reasons for this popularity? Is your area popular with domestic holidaymakers? Discuss with your group. C

The map statistics were included in *Social Trends* 1998. These statistics show that domestic tourists prefer different areas to overseas tourists visiting the UK. For instance, London was only chosen for 2% of domestic visitors, whereas 53% of overseas visitors selected London.

CASE STUDY

Tourism in Wales

In 1995 it was estimated that more than 9% of all employment in Wales (95,000 jobs) were due to tourism, more than 60,000 of them serving tourists directly in tourism-related industries and more than 30,000 of them in industries supplying tourism.

	TRIPS (m)	NIGHTS (m)	EXPENDITURE (£m)
Domestic (UK) tourism 1995	10.4	43.2	1,044
Overseas tourism 1995 (P)	0.736	5.3	197
Leisure day visits 1995 (E)	45	–	360

(P) Provisional, (E) Estimated

TABLE 7 *Volume and value of tourism in Wales 1995*

	TRIPS		NIGHTS		EXPENDITURE	
	(m)	%	(m)	%	(£)	%
All tourism	10.4	100	43.2	100	1,044	100
Holidays	6.7	64	33.1	77	865	83
Holidays 1 to 3 nights	2.7	26	5.8	14	174	17
Holidays 4+ nights	4.0	38	27.3	63	691	66
Visits to friends and family	2.5	24	6.1	14	57	5
Business	0.8	8	2.3	5	101	10
Other purposes	0.4	4	1.6	4	19	2

TABLE 8 *Purpose of visit to Wales by domestic (UK) visitors 1995*

	ALL TOURISM TRIPS (%)	ALL HOLIDAY TRIPS (%)
Private car	82	87
Hired car	1	1
Regular bus/coach	3	2
Coach tour	3	3
Train	5	4
Other	6	3

TABLE 9 *Main type of transport used by domestic (UK) visitors to Wales 1995*

ACCOMMODATION USED	ALL TOURISM TRIPS (%)	ALL HOLIDAY TRIPS (%)
Hotel/motel/guest house	15	15
Rented accommodation	7	11
Hostel/university/school	1	1
Bed and breakfast	2	3
Farmhouse	1	1
Friends/relatives home	38	22
Camping	7	10
Towed caravan	4	7
Static caravan	17	26
Holiday camp/village	3	4
Other	6	5

TABLE 10 *Accommodation used by domestic (UK) visitors to Wales 1995*

ORIGIN OF TRIP (GB STANDARD REGION)	ALL TOURISM TRIPS (%)	ALL HOLIDAY TRIPS (%)
North	1	2
Yorkshire/Humberside	3	3
North West	17	22
East Midlands	4	5
West Midlands	17	21
East Anglia	1	1
South East	18	18
South West	9	8
Wales	28	18
Scotland	1	1
Northern Ireland	*	*

*Less than 0.5%

TABLE 11 *Region of residence of domestic (UK) visitors to Wales 1995*

Source for tables 7–11: Wales Tourist Board website

ACTIVITY

In tables 7–11 above you will notice that the domestic market for Wales' tourism is much higher than the overseas (incoming) market. Examine these tables and prepare a short report on:

1. The main source of the visitors to Wales.

2. The main purpose of the visit.

3. The preferred mode of transport and accommodation.

Summarise your findings giving reasons for the results. Ⓒ Ⓝ ⒤⒯

At least we get the beach to ourselves at home

Outgoing tourism

The UK travel industry is very sophisticated and travel agents have been sending British holidaymakers abroad since the mid-19th century. Thomas Cook was the first travel agent to offer inclusive tours in this country and abroad, and Sir Henry Lunn introduced skiing holidays at about the same time.

The term 'package holiday' was only introduced in the early 1960s when the first inclusive tour by air was arranged by Horizon Holidays to Corsica. Until then tours were arranged by coach and rail. The British took 29 million holidays overseas in 1997, and spent £17,220 million (see Table 12).

Travel and tourism in the UK is highly developed and covers a wide range of activities, facilities and services, made available through a variety of suppliers. These key components all fit together to provide travellers and tourists with essential services (see page 48).

Travel agents

There are over 7000 travel agents in the UK who are members of the Association of British Travel Agents (ABTA) and many more who belong to other professional organisations which also serve to protect the customer.

There are several types of travel agent. The most commonly recognised are the retail agents which are found in town and city centres. These are divided into independent and multiple agencies. Independent agencies are often family owned and offer a wider range of services than the multiple agencies. Generally they compete well with the larger multiples as they offer a personal service and are able to sell any tour operator's products, whereas a multiple agency usually only offers a limited range. However, multiples are able to offer better discounts as they have stronger purchasing power. Many of the multiples are owned by tour operators and only offer their own company's products. Some of the main multiple agencies are: World Choice, First Choice, Thomsons, Going Places, Co-op Travelcare.

Both independent and multiple travel agencies are able to offer:

- leisure and business travel booking arrangements by air, coach and rail
- cruises
- supplies of foreign currency
- coach holidays

ACTIVITY

Which is the most popular destination in Table 12? What do you think are the reasons this destination is so popular? Discuss your favourite destination. Ⓒ Ⓝ 🗩

(PERCENTAGES)	1971	1981	1991	1997
Spain[2]	34.3	21.7	21.3	26.3
France	15.9	27.2	25.8	23.1
United States	1.0	5.5	6.8	6.7
Greece	4.5	6.7	7.6	4.7
Italy	9.2	5.8	3.5	4.2
Portugal	2.6	2.8	4.8	4.0
Irish Republic	–	3.6	3.0	3.6
Turkey	–	0.1	0.7	3.1
Netherlands	3.6	2.4	3.5	2.8
Cyprus	1.0	0.7	2.4	2.2
Belgium	–	2.1	2.1	2.2
Germany	3.4	2.6	2.7	1.7
Malta	–	2.6	1.7	1.2
Austria	5.5	2.5	2.4	1.1
Other countries	19.0	13.7	11.8	13.2
All destinations (= 100%) (thousands)	4,201	13,131	20,788	29,138

[1] A visit made for holiday purposes. Business trips and visits to friends or relatives are excluded.
[2] Excludes the Canary Islands prior to 1981.

TABLE 12 *Holidays abroad: by destination.*   *Source: International Passenger Survey, Office for National Statistics*

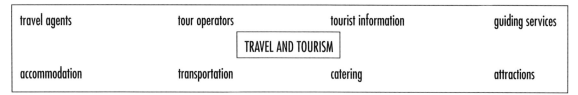

travel agents	tour operators	tourist information	guiding services
	TRAVEL AND TOURISM		
accommodation	transportation	catering	attractions

The components of travel and tourism

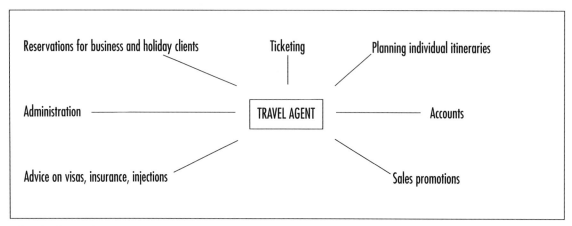

The role of a travel agent

Depending on the type of licences they have, these agencies can also: book air tickets, make car ferry bookings, reserve express coach seats, arrange care hire or book rail tickets.

Franchised agencies have also opened in the last ten years. These offer the best of the multiple's purchasing power with the personal touch. A 'franchisee' buys the franchise from a large group of travel agents; this gives it the right to use the group's name, logo, stationery etc. Uniglobe is one such agency. Other examples of franchises in the leisure and tourism industry are: Pizza Hut, KFC and Holiday Inn.

Many of these small independent agencies have formed into their own groups (or 'consortia'), to enable them to have the purchasing power of the multiples, and be able to offer the same discounts.

Travel agents earn an income by commission which they receive from the 'principals' whose products they sell. Principals are: tour and rail operators, airlines, shipping, insurance, care hire and coach companies. Agents can also make money on travellers' cheques and foreign exchange, on money they hold on deposit for holidays, and by selling ancillary services such as ski packages. If they arrange individual itineraries for customers, they can add a 'mark up' or arrangement fee. Some agencies also arrange their own inclusive tours. Agents can also charge for services such as obtaining visas.

ACTIVITY

Find out how many travel agencies operate in your locality. List them as independent, multiples and franchised. Ⓒ

Tour operators

Tour operators put together the various components of inclusive holidays and put them in a 'package' in a brochure at an all-inclusive price.

Brochures are usually distributed and the holidays sold through travel agents, but increasingly customers are going directly to the operator either by selecting holidays through teletext on television or the Internet. Some operators only sell directly by post. They obtain their customers by extensive advertising. Two of the major tour operators in the UK are Thomson and Airtours. They cater for the mass market and carry most of the UK tourists going abroad. However, there are also thousands of smaller operators who specialise in different types of holidays, such as:

- for a particular age group (Saga for over 50s, The Club for 18–30 year olds)
- for a single country destination (Magic of Italy, Citalia, Manos)
- self-catering only (Meon Villa, Villa Select, Britanny Holidays)
- camping (Eurosites, Sunsites)

- special interest (Cox and Kings, Silkcut)
- cruises (Cunard, Princess, P and O)
- flight only (Unijet, Jetsave, easyJet)

The components of an inclusive tour are bought by the tour operator and then added together to form the complete package.

A tour operator will, for example, either own its own airline or will purchase seats from an airline (charter them), purchase passenger handling services at the airports, hire coaches to transfer passengers to accommodation, which they have booked and appoint resort staff to look after the passengers during their holiday.

There are also many tour operators offering holidays by coach and rail and for customers who wish to use their own car.

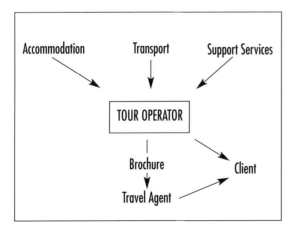

The role of the tour operator and travel agent in selling holidays

ACTIVITY

1. **Compare two general tour operators' brochures for the same resort. Compare the types of accommodation offered, and the cost of the holidays. You should make the comparison between holidays to the same type of accommodation, from the same departure airport, at the same time of year and for the same duration.**

2. **Compare two specialist or coach operators' products in the same way.**

3. **In pairs, role play travel agents selecting and pricing holidays for each other.**

Accommodation	Transportation	Support Services
hotels	charter flights	resort representatives
guest houses	schedule flights	transfer representatives
pensions	coach	children's representatives
gites	car ferry	activity organisers
bed and breakfast	rail	excursions
chalets	taxi	car hire
cabins	car	ski hire
caravans	motorhome	tour guides
tents	cruise liner	sports coaches/instructors
motorhomes	gulet	
hotel boats	charter yachts	
longboats	river cruise boats	
motor cruisers	longboats	
apartments and villas	motor cruisers	
tavernas, private homes, hostels		

The components of an inclusive tour. Note that some of the components are featured in more than one category.

Tourist information centres and guiding services

Tourist information centres in the UK are operated by local authorities or the tourist boards. They offer information on both the local area and the whole country. Depending on the number of overseas visitors, the staff may need to speak several languages. At one time the tourist information staff at Stratford upon Avon were able to offer 17 languages between them! Some tourist information centres are only opened during the summer season.

The restructuring of the tourist boards in the UK has led to the introduction of ABTA as a leading body for ensuring the quality of tourist information centres. The general public are accustomed to using ABTA approved and bonded travel agencies for their overseas holidays and so it was logical that the same system should be adopted to cover holidays booked in the UK, either through travel agencies or the Tourist Information Centres (TICs). The first TIC to gain such approval was in Leicester.

Local information centres often act as an information point for local residents, providing information on schools, local services, housing, as well as visitor attractions and entertainment venues.

Leicester TIC signs up with ABTA

LEICESTER'S tourist information centre has become the first in the country to be granted ABTA membership for its UK holiday shop, a commercial division of Leicester Promotions.

The shop began trading last summer. Manager Josie Martino said: 'For most people, a holiday is the highlight of their year. ABTA bonding will give customers that extra confidence that everything will run as smoothly as possible.

'They can now be fully confident the holiday shop business is financially sound, brochure descriptions are accurate, that staff will handle bookings with the highest standards of quality and care and that their money is safe.'

ABTA president Steven Freudmann said: 'We have worked for many years with domestic tourist bodies on joint initiatives which encourage those who want to stay in this country to make the most of their opportunities.

'To do this effectively, holidaymakers are increasingly turning to travel agencies and tourism offices.'

Source: Travel GBI

Transportation

Flights for inclusive holidays are generally charter, that means the whole flight has been booked by one or more tour operators, for the use of their passengers only. Charter flights can be changed at the last minute, or even cancelled if there is insufficient demand. Some of the most well known charter airlines are: Britannia (owned by Thomsons), Airtours and Cosmos.

Some of the more expensive operators include scheduled airline tickets in their tours. These have to operate as their licence is only granted if they keep to their schedule and usually there is more flexibility for passengers or businesses on schedule flight times. Passengers can also choose to fly first class if they wish.

Other types of transport are included in inclusive tours:

- It is possible to book a fly-drive holiday, where the tour includes return flights to a destination and then a hire car or motorhome for the length of the holiday. This appeals to independent travellers who wish to tour around an area. Motorhomes

are particularly popular in the USA and Australia where they are called 'recreational vehicles' – RVs for short (see Case Study on page 52).

- You can book your car on a car ferry and prebook accommodation for a motoring tour, for example though France or Spain. This gives the customer peace of mind that they will have accommodation booked throughout their tour, and the rate negotiated by a tour operator is usually cheaper than an independent traveller can obtain. There is also added security in the support which the tour operator can offer in the case of any problems.

Other methods of transport

The Eurotunnel has been slow to gain customers, but is gaining is popularity now and is the fastest way to reach France from the UK either by taking a car or going on the train.

Motorail, where the car is loaded onto the train, is also a popular way of travelling, especially over long distances.

CASE STUDY

A typical fly-drive holiday
FLY-DRIVES in POUSADAS, HOTELS and MANOR HOUSES

Portugal is a small country with many fascinating aspects, ideal for a fly-drive holiday enabling you to see the places of interest at your own pace. Cars are provided on an unlimited mileage basis, collected at the airport on arrival and left at the airport on departure: any combination of Faro, Lisbon or Porto airports may be used, depending on the itinerary decided upon. We have selected our accommodation in towns of character affording access to nearby points of special interest, but please bear in mind that the town hotels are not necessarily in secluded or quiet locations. Several itineraries using Pousadas, Hotels or a mixture of Manor Houses and

Hotels are suggested on this page, to give an idea of the scope and price range available.

But, please feel free to plan your own route – we are only too pleased to help. Don't forget you can combine just about all our holidays: spend a week in a resort and another touring, book accommodation for one week and car for two weeks, complement a fly-drive itinerary with several nights in selected Pousadas and Manor Houses – with a stay in the Azores or Madeira or on the Estoril/Cascais coast affording easy access to Lisbon.

POUSADA FLY DRIVE ITINERARIES

We suggest two 7 and 14 night itineraries and one 10 night, though any number of nights between 7 and 28 can be arranged. However, we must warn clients that early booking is imperative, and itineraries may well have to be altered slightly if some Pousadas are fully booked. We are also able to tailormake any itinerary/length of stay required on scheduled TAP flights, flying into one airport and out of another.

FPOUS 1–7 nights (flying into Faro, out of Lisbon)
1 night Sagres (R)
1 night Alvito/Beja (H)
1 night Evora (H)
1 night Estremoz (H)
1 night Obidos (H)
2 nights Palmela/Setubal (H)

FPOUS 2–7 nights (flying into and out or Porto)
2 nights Murtosa (R)
1 night Amarante (R)
1 night Canicada (R)
1 night Vila Nova de Cerveira (R)
2 nights Guimaraes (H)

FPOUS 3–10 nights (flying into and out of Lisbon)
2 nights Queluz (H)
2 nights Sines (R)
2 nights Estremoz (H)
2 nights Marvao (R)
2 nights Obidos (H)

FPOUS 4–14 nights (flying into Faro, out of Porto)
1 night S. Bras (R)
2 nights Sines (R)
1 night Serpa (R)
2 nights Sousel (R)
2 nights Tomar (R)
2 nights Manteigas (R)
2 nights Almeida (R)
2 nights Amarante (R)

FPOUS 5–14 nights (flying into Lisbon, out of Porto)
2 nights Palmela/Setubal (H)
2 nights Estremoz (H)
1 night Obidos (H)
1 night Povoa das Quartas (R)
2 nights Miranda do Douro (R)
2 nights Canicada (R)
2 nights Viana do Castelo (R)
2 nights Amares (H)

NOTE: The letter by the Pousada denotes its grade. We have suggested itineraries based on either cheaper or more expensive Pousadas so as to suit every pocket. Prices are based on two persons sharing a twin room on bed and breakfast and a Group 'A' car. You can combine the Pousadas with Hotels, Manor Houses and Quintas. Plan your itinerary and ask us to price it for you.

The letters H/R indicate the category to which each Pousada belongs.
Type H (generally deluxe accommodation)
Type R (generally more standard accommodation 3 to 4 star).
NOTE: From time to time Pousadas close for renovation.

Ⓡ Denotes Pousada (Regional) Ⓗ Denotes Pousada (Historical)
◻ Denotes Manor House/Quinta

Source: Sunvil Discovery

Ferry Operator's Traffic Hit By Chunnel

April 30, 1996

LONDON (AP) – The biggest ferry operator on the English Channel said on Tuesday that automobile and passenger traffic was hurt dramatically early this year by competition from the Channel Tunnel.

P&O European Ferries said it carried 292,780 tourist vehicles, a drop of 23%, on the key route between Dover, England, and Calais, France, during the first three months of 1996.

The number of P&O passengers on the route fell by 17% to nearly 1.6 million as the 'Chunnel', operated by Eurotunnel, took its bite out of one of the most lucrative transportation markets in Europe. P&O said fares also fell because of competition from Eurotunnel, but would not disclose revenues.

P&O said Eurotunnel's share of the market had risen to about 40% from 20%, although Eurotunnel puts its figure in the mid-40s.

Eurotunnel last week reported that its losses more than doubled in 1995, its first full year of business, even as revenue shot up to 299 million pounds, or $464 million, from 30.6 million pounds.

Last year, Eurotunnel went into default on interest payments to bankers who are owed about 8 billion pounds ($12.4 billion). The company and its banks are seeking a solution to the debt crisis, which could result in the banks owning a stake.

Source: http://sddt.com/files/librarywire

The car ferry companies have responded to the competition posed by the Eurotunnel by introducing super ferries which are more like cruise liners, and huge catamarans which halve the time taken to cross the Channel.

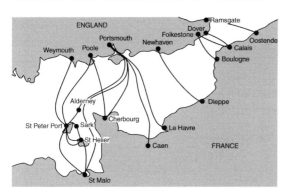

Ferry routes to mainland Europe and the Channel Isles

Source: Travel Trade Gazette

Coach tours have a steady number of customers, usually in the older age group, but the budget tours, when coaches travel overnight across Europe, provide a cheap way for young people to travel. Some of the most popular coach tour destinations abroad are: to Venice, Florence and Rome in Italy, and to Madrid, Seville and Granada in Spain. There is always a steady demand for the Lakes and Mountains of Switzerland, Austria and Italy, and coach operators offer many short breaks to Paris, Amsterdam, Brussels and also to events such as the Belgian Beer Festival or Tulip season in Holland.

Cruising around the Mediterranean, the Caribbean or around the world is an ambition for most people. Anniversaries, birthdays and retirements are often celebrated with a cruise, and it is the type of holiday most people dream of taking if they win the lottery. However, some of the world cruises book up several years ahead! Although they appear to be expensive, the fact that all meals, accommodation, transport and entertainment are included in the price means that a cruise offers good value for money. The cruise market in the UK is mostly aimed at older people, but in the USA short cruises are popular with all ages.

The introduction of cheaper air fares has led to the introduction of 'fly-cruises', enabling passengers to fly to the embarkation port and then cruise. This cuts out the long transatlantic crossing for cruises to the Caribbean and is a quicker way to reach the southern Mediterranean. Fly-cruises are offered by the large cruise line companies and also by tour operators.

A cross channel: 'super ferry': The SuperStar Express
Source: © P&O European Ferries (Portsmouth) Ltd.

Century – Western Tropical Adventure (10–19 December 1999)

Itinerary:

Friday	**UK/Miami**	fly to Miami and transfer to first class overnight hotel.
Saturday	**Miami**	transfer to Port Everglades and embark on Century.
Sunday	**At Sea**	cruising the Caribbean.
Monday	**Ocho Rios, Jamaica**	climb the 600 feet high Dunn's River Falls or just lay back with a rum punch – 'no problem!'
Tuesday	**Grand Cayman**	a chance to experience incredible snorkelling and diving, plus Seven Mile Beach.
Wednesday	**Cozumel, Mexico**	visit the mysterious Mayan ruins of Tulum.
Thursday		cruising back to the USA.
Friday	**Key West**	America's own 'Caribbean Isle' at the very tip of the Florida Keys.
Saturday	**Miami**	arrive at Port Everglades; day at leisure with use of hotel facilities; transfer to airport for return flight.
Sunday	**UK**	early morning arrival in the UK.

Please note: Shore excursions are not included in the package price and are suggestions only.

Grand Restaurant

Aquaspa

A typical fly-cruise itinerary for Celebrity Cruises

Source: Air Miles cruise club magazine

Other methods of transport you need to investigate are the rail and coach services. National Express is a major coach operator in the UK, offering routes across the whole of the country. Coach travel is still the most economical means of transport.

Rail travel has become very expensive, especially since the railways were privatised. There have also been problems caused by the ownership of the railway system being shared by smaller companies, which has led to some difficulties for travellers when trying to find out information about timetables or fares.

ACTIVITY

Choose a destination for a day visit from your home area and find out the fares by rail and coach. Plan an itinerary showing times of departure, arrival and other features of importance to a traveller, such as change over points. If possible, print out the itinerary using a word processor.

Car hire services are available worldwide and many independent travellers prefer to collect a hire car at their destination airport or railway station, rather than rely on public transport. There are many car hire companies, but the most well-known are probably Hertz, Avis and Budget. Tariffs for car hire vary from country to country.

ACTIVITY

Obtain some car hire brochures (or use holiday brochures) and calculate the cost of hiring the same type of car with each company, in one destination. Compare your findings.

Accommodation and catering

There is a wide range of accommodation available to tourists in the UK and abroad. As shown below, 50% of UK residents holidaying abroad are likely to use self-catering accommodation.

ACTIVITY

Compare the types of accommodation used in Wales in the earlier part of this chapter, with those used abroad. How do they compare? Can you explain the reasons for any differences?

CLASSIFICATION OF ACCOMMODATION

To help customers to choose accommodation, there are various classification schemes. In the UK, each tourist board has its own scheme. In England, the English Tourism Council has joined with the Automobile Association (A.A.) and the Royal Automobile Club (R.A.C.) to create one overall rating scheme for Hotels and Guest

(PERCENTAGES)	1971	1981	1991	1996
Hotel/motel	67	59	47	46
Rented villa/flat	4	10	23	22
Friend's/relative's home	20	19	20	21
Boat	4	3	3	4
Pension/boarding/guest house	4	3	3	3
Own house/villa	–	3	4	3
Camping	6	6	3	2
Caravan	2	3	2	2
Youth hostel	1	1	1	2
Holiday camp/village	1	1	1	1
Other	4	4	5	7

[1] Holidays of four nights or more taken by Great Britain residents aged 16 and over. Percentages add to more than 100 as more than one type of accommodation could have been used.

TABLE 13 *Type of accommodation used on holidays[1] abroad.*

Source: British National Travel Survey, British Tourist Authority

House Accommodation. This scheme has replaced the old 'crown symbol' and uses stars and diamonds. Stars (from one to five) are used to indicate the quality of the accommodation, the level of service, the range of facilities and standard of food provided in hotels, and diamonds (also from one to five) indicate the quality of other types of accommodation, such as pubs, farmhouses, and private homes offering bed and breakfast. The ratings are assessed by a team of inspectors who visit the accommodation anonymously.

Accommodation abroad is also classified, usually by the number of stars on display, but each country also has its own method of assessing quality. Some countries, for example, will award higher stars for good public facilities, such as lifts, or large reception areas. Yet the guest accommodation is perhaps not so high a standard or there may not be a restaurant. Aiming for a lower grading can also have tax advantages in some countries, so you could for instance, find that the hotel has chosen not to offer a service, and therefore, go down a category.

UK Tour Operators have great difficulty in showing hotels in different countries in their brochures. A four star hotel in one country

YOUR GUIDE TO
STAYING HAPPY
THE NEW GUEST ACCOMMODATION RATINGS EXPLAINED

Our Diamond ratings reflect visitor expectations, whereby quality is seen as more important than facilities and services.
Guest Accommodation is required to meet progressively higher standards of quality and guest care as they move up the scale from one to five Diamonds.

 Clean and comfortable. A full cooked or continental breakfast. Other meals where provided, must be freshly prepared. Clean bed linen, towels and fresh soap. Adequate heating, with hot water available at reasonable times for bathing or showers, at no extra cost. An acceptable overall level of quality and helpful service.

 All the above plus, a higher level of quality and comfort with greater emphasis on guest care in all areas.

All the above plus, a good overall level of quality. Well maintained, practical décor. A good choice of dishes for breakfast. All other meals where provided, will be freshly prepared using quality ingredients. A greater degree of comfort and guest care.

All the above plus, a very good level of quality and comfort. A very good degree of guest care, and extra attention given to cleanliness and warmth of welcome.

All the above plus, an excellent overall level of quality and comfort with ample space and a degree of luxury. A fine quality bed, high quality furniture and interior design. A high proportion of bedrooms with en-suite or private facilities. Other meals where available, made with fresh, seasonal local ingredients. Excellent levels of guest care.

YOUR GUIDE TO
STAYING HAPPY
THE NEW HOTEL RATINGS EXPLAINED

Our Star ratings symbolise the level of service, range of facilities and quality of guest care that you can expect. Hotels are required to meet progressively higher standards as they move up the scale from one to five Stars.

 High standard of cleanliness. Limited range of facilities and services. Friendly and helpful staff. Restaurant/eating area open to you and your guests for breakfast and dinner. A bar or lounge serving alcohol. 75% of bedrooms with en-suite or private facilities.

 All the above plus, better equipped and more comfortable accommodation. All bedrooms with en-suite or private facilities and colour TV. A straight forward range of services with a more personal touch. Food and drink is of a slightly higher standard. A lift is normally available.

All the above plus, greater quality and a higher standard of services and facilities. Usually larger hotels with more spacious public areas and bedrooms. A more formal style of service. Room service of continental breakfast. Laundry service. Greater attention to quality of food.

All the above plus, superior comfort and quality. All bedrooms with en-suite facilities, both bath and shower and WC. More emphasis on quality food and drink. Skilled staff anticipating and responding to needs and requests. Room service of all meals. 24hr drinks and snacks.

All the above plus, luxurious and spacious surroundings. The highest international quality of accommodation, services and a range of extra facilities. Professional, attentive, highly trained staff. Superb cuisine. Striking décor. Exceptional comfort. Sophisticated ambience.

The new ETC classification scheme

Source: English Tourism Council

might only warrant two stars in another. To make it easier for the customer to compare hotels across the different countries in a brochure, large operators, such as Thomson and Cosmos, have introduced their own categories.

The National Tourist Boards' information centres are responsible for distributing information to incoming groups, and marketing the UK abroad and only have offices in the capitals in the UK and large centres abroad.

Guiding services cover public, voluntary and private sectors. For instance, a National Trust property may have volunteer house guides, a

ACTIVITY

1. Discuss the two hotel descriptions below, taken from a Cosmos Winter Sun Brochure. Can you identify why the Hotel Florida has been awarded three diamonds and the Hotel Esmeralda Playa has been classified as four diamonds? 🗨

2. Compare the descriptions and diamond ratings of these two hotels with another tour operator's classification scheme. Ⓒ

Diamond ratings

To help you choose the right accommodation, all hotels and apartments in this brochure have been awarded a Cosmos 'Diamond Rating'. This is based on our own personal knowledge of each property (at the time of going to press) as well as your own views. Ratings range from 2 diamonds for basic value-for-money accommodation up to 5 diamonds for properties where you can expect excellent facilities and extra touches of comfort. We also feature ratings of 2½, 3½ and 4½ diamonds.

Hotel Esmeralda Playa ◆ ◆ ◆ ◆

The Esmeralda Playa is ideal for a winter break. It is equipped with a host of amenities and entertainment, and stands only 200 metres from the beach.
FACILITIES • 2 pools (1 heated) with sunbeds and parasols • Lifts
MEALS AND DRINKS • Restaurant • A la carte menu available • Buffet-style breakfast and dinner • Pool bar • Lounge bar • Supplement for: Full board
ENTERTAINMENT • Day and evening entertainment programme including shows, live music and flamenco
SPORTS • Table tennis • Squash and tennis courts (equipment for hire) • Minigolf • Pool table • Sauna, jacuzzi
FUN FOR KIDS • Separate children's pool • Playroom • Hotel children's club (4 to 10 years, Dec to Apr only) • **Free** cots
CHILD PRICES AND FREE PLACES: 2 to 12 years
ACCOMMODATION: Prices are based on half board in a twin room with bath and w.c. Balcony and side sea view. Supplement for: Single room.
(Fridge/minibar, safety deposit box and TV payable locally).
OFFICIAL RATING: 4 star
303 bedrooms

Hotel Florida ◆ ◆ ◆

- FREE Mystery Tour
- FREE Tea and biscuits daily
- Complimentary Welcome drink
- Cards and board games
- Golden Times library
- Guided walk around your resort

SITUATION: The Florida is separated from the sea front promenade and beach by its attractive garden and pool area. It is also right near the centre of town with its shops, cafes and bars and is ideally positioned for exploring Fuengirola. The hotel has an elegant, comfortable style, and the atmosphere is warm and inviting.
AMENITIES: Emphasis is on peace and relaxation in the Florida. There's a comfortable lounge and bar overlooking the separate garden and terrace with its two outdoor pools, one of which is solar heated. Here the open bar serves drinks and snacks in warmer weather. Indoors there's a separate lounge with satellite TV channels, but you can also watch TV in your bedroom or just take a book to the quiet room. All bedrooms have safety deposit boxes available at extra charge. The hotel is centrally heated.
MEALS: are taken in the small restaurant off the lounge. Dinner is waiter service, buffet-style hot cooked breakfast.
PRICES: are based on half board in a twin room with bath and w.c.
SUPPLEMENTS: (per person per night) Single room with shower, w.c. £5.20 No supplement for departures on 5 Dec (7 & 14 nights) and 12 Dec (7 nights). Full board £3.60. (Nil in residence 1–30 Nov & 5 Jan–13 Feb.)
REDUCTIONS: (per night) 3rd adult sharing a room £2.00.
OFFICIAL RATING: 3 Star
NO. OF ROOMS: 116

Source: Cosmos Winter Sun brochure

Logos for the English Tourism Council and the Northern Ireland Tourist Board

local authority-owned museum will employ guides and tour operators employ local guides to accompany groups on sightseeing tours.

ACTIVITY

Visit the tourist information centre in your chosen area and note the types of information provided. How knowledgeable are the staff? Do they speak any foreign languages? C

Links between leisure and tourism

Throughout this chapter many references have been made to the links across the different sectors and components of the leisure and tourism industry. In order to offer the widest choice of facilities, and good quality services, these links are essential. For example, consider all the steps in booking a holiday. You will need:

- to select the holiday from a brochure supplied by a travel agent or Tourist

Information Centre (tour operator, travel agent, printers)
- transport to the destination (bus, air, taxi, train, ferry, car)
- foreign currency and travel insurance (bank, exchange office)
- visa and health information (cmbassy, doctor)
- accommodation (from hotels to pensions)
- help in the resort (resort representative or guide, sports instructors)
- luggage (clothes, electrical equipment, sun lotions, guide books)

Some of the providers of these services will be in the public, private or voluntary sector.

ACTIVITY

As a group, try to identify as many links as possible between the following, which are essential to a known leisure or tourism facility:

- **transport**
- **catering**
- **visitor attractions**
- **tourist information providers**
- **suppliers of goods related to leisure and tourism**
- **accommodation**
- **tour organisers**
- **public, private and voluntary sectors**
- **media**
- **local services, such as fire, accident or health** C

PORTFOLIO TASK

Prepare a guidebook or presentation on a selected area. Your guide should:

✓ **provide a clear description of the leisure and tourism industries in the area**

✓ **describe two leisure and tourism organisations for each component, using technical terms correctly, including details on their sector, activities and facilities**

✓ **describe three links between leisure and tourism organisations**

✓ **describe two examples of links between leisure and tourism organisations in different sectors**

✓ **describe the products and services of the two major facilities you have identified.**

In addition, you should:

✓ **write a definition of leisure and tourism**

✓ **make a short report comparing and contrasting the products and services offered by the two major facilities**

✓ **describe how leisure and tourism facilities in the area could work together to improve the products and services they provide**

✓ **identify any gaps in the provision of these services and make recommendations as to how they could be addressed.**

Include a list of all sources of information used, with an explanation of why you selected the sources and mentioning any you rejected as unsuitable.

Completion of this Portfolio Task should enable you to gather partial evidence for the following **key skills**:

C2.2 Read and summarise information

C2.3 Write 2 different types of document about straightforward subjects

IT2.1 Search for and select information for 2 different purposes.

IT2.2 Explore and develop information (if a computer is used).

IT2.3 Present combined information for 2 different purposes (if a computer is used).

C H A P T E R 4

Marketing and promotion in leisure and tourism

What do you understand by the term 'marketing'? Have you or your friends ever been persuaded to buy something which you have seen advertised on television or in a magazine? Would you have bought it anyway, or were you persuaded to buy the article because of the advertisement? The use of clever marketing and promotion activities ensures that many leisure and tourism goods and services are sold to the public successfully. Consider the huge demand for certain brand names of leisure wear – how did they become so successful, and why do so many young people demand only certain names? The reason is because of the sustained marketing efforts of the companies concerned.

These goods and services are not essential items, they are bought when a customer has some surplus income available to spend on leisure clothes and activities such as sport or travelling. Therefore leisure and tourism organisations have to compete very strongly to ensure that this surplus is spent on *their* products and not those of the competition.

Marketing has been defined as 'the management process which identifies, anticipates and supplies customer requirements efficiently and profitably'.

From this definition you will see that there are several components to marketing:

- identifying customer needs
- anticipating customer requirements to meet those needs, and
- supplying the appropriate goods efficiently and profitably

Identifying customer needs

This is the first essential step in marketing. The term 'leisure and tourism products' covers a very wide variety of actual goods such as sports and hobby equipment, and services such as selling holidays and leisure activities.

Companies have to carry out research to identify customers' needs before they even start to develop a new product or service and plan their marketing campaigns. This can be carried out in a variety of ways including:

- interviewing current and potential users of the products
- studying the competition
- trial offers

By interviewing customers who use a competitor's product, the company can also anticipate any changes desired by the customers and whether a new product would sell. The research would identify the price the public would be prepared to pay for a new product and whether the choice of brand name would appeal to the public. This is called primary (or field) research. No doubt you or your friends have been asked to fill in a questionnaire sometime either by someone in a shopping centre or at your front door. Occasionally these surveys are carried out by telephone or post. Many companies use a questionnaire after a customer has received their service not only to check on customer satisfaction, but also to gather information about future needs of a customer, e.g. new products, such as holiday destinations.

Marketing is used to decide whether there is demand for a product (either new or modified), whether it would sell, and the price that would be acceptable to the public. It is then used to promote and distribute the product.

 CASE STUDY

Happy Times Ltd wanted to develop children's play areas in major shopping centres. They carried out research in centres asking parents what they would want from such an area. The parents' main requirements were:

- a safe secure and healthy environment
- low cost
- entertaining for children
- easily accessible
- open during main shopping hours

The company decided to obtain sites near to the largest supermarkets in the centres, employ fully qualified nursery nurses, have a link with the nearest medical centre, provide a secure checking in and checking out system, and provide car parking spaces. Local drama groups and entertainers were engaged to provide different activities every day, such as face painting, juggling, dressing up, making balloon animals. The entrance fees were to be subsidised by the local supermarkets who realised they would gain more shoppers if there was somewhere safe for them to leave their children.

Target marketing

Once a company has identified that there is a need for a new product or service, they then have to decide how to promote that service. This is done by 'target marketing', i.e. the customer has to be identified and placed in different categories or 'segments'. These segments can be determined by:

- age group
- gender
- social group
- lifestyle
- ethnicity

It is fairly easy to recognise that the needs of different age groups will vary widely and that to a certain extent there are some differences between the needs of males and females. However, classifying people according to their social grouping is more complicated.

A traditional method of classifying people is to use the 'Head of Household's' employment as a guide, as this was supposed to indicate the type of lifestyle that the whole family would follow. However, this is becoming less and less reliable in the changing world of work and the fact that not all members of a family may adopt the same buying patterns. Table 14 shows how this system identified customers. Newspapers will refer to their readers by this classification, to indicate to advertisers the type of readers they have. You will see that as a student you are classified as Social Grade 'E', but if your father or mother is a judge, then you would immediately change to Grade 'A'.

As this system is too rigid, various other methods of classification are also used including life cycle and lifestyle classifications. The life cycle classification is a good indicator of suitable customers for leisure and tourism and has nine categories (see Table 15).

SOCIAL GRADE	SOCIAL CLASS	TYPICAL OCCUPATIONS
A	Upper middle	Higher managerial, admin. and professional (e.g. judges, surgeons)
B	Middle	Intermediate managerial and admin. (e.g. lawyers, teachers, doctors)
C1	Lower middle	Supervisory, clerical, junior management (e.g. bank clerk, estate agent)
C2	Skilled working	Skilled manual workers (e.g. joiner, welder)
D	Working	Semi- and unskilled manual workers (e.g. driver, postman, porter)
E	Those at lowest level of subsistence	Pensioners, widows, casual workers, students, the unemployed

TABLE 14 *Socio-economic classification*

CATEGORY	CHARACTERISTICS
1 Bachelor stage	Young singles, reasonable level of disposable income, which is mostly spent on entertainment, such as pubs, discos, CDs, computer games.
2 Newly-weds/living together	Maybe slightly higher income spent on eating out, clubbing, cinemas.
3 Full nest 1	Young couples with child under six years. Main leisure pursuits would be related to family outings.
4 Full nest 2	Young couples with youngest child over six years. Less disposable income to spend on leisure.
5 Full nest 3	Older couple with dependent children, possibly students. Little disposable income.
6 Empty nest 1	Childless couple or children left home. Disposable income has increased, likely to pursue more frequent holidays, active leisure pursuits, such as golf, tennis.
7 Empty nest 2	Older couples. Chief earner retired. Entertainment home-based.
8 Solitary survivor 1	Single/widowed working person. Mostly home-based entertainment.
9 Solitary survivor 2	Retired single person. Little disposable income for leisure purposes.

TABLE 15 *Life cycle classification*

LIFESTYLE CLASSIFICATION

A lifestyle classification is used to identify the different types of need. The method usually used refers to four classes of people:

- **Mainstreamers** – The largest of the four groups, recognised as representing 40% of the British population. These people stick to well-known makes and brands and have very conventional leisure pursuits, such as gardening, reading or walking.
- **Aspirers** – These people are often self-employed, and like to have the latest status symbols, such as expensive jewellery or the latest fashions. They are likely to enjoy all the latest adult 'toys', such as hang-gliders or water jet-skis.
- **Succeeders** – These people have already arrived at a certain status and no longer need to impress others. They like quality products and are likely to enjoy entertaining visitors, socialising and playing golf, and taking frequent short breaks.
- **Reformers** – This group tends to be the best educated and the least interested in material goods. They are more likely to

provide their own entertainment in leisure time by reading, camping or cycling, for example. They sometimes belong to pressure groups such as 'Greenpeace'.

The special needs of people from different ethnic backgrounds is also an essential part of marketing research. Some activities might not be allowed and some services, such as catering, may need special attention for religious reasons. Other considerations include the type of promotions and advertising that may or may not be allowed in different countries. Careful use of language is essential and even the choice of certain colours can be offensive.

ACTIVITY

Study a variety of advertisements and identify which socio-economic, life cycle or lifestyle category is being targeted for each advertisement. Discuss with a partner.

Market research is also used to identify the target markets for a company's products. For instance, an airline might be targeting:

- first class passengers
- club class or business passengers
- economy class passengers
- charter groups
- last minute bookers

Similarly, a tourist attraction might be aiming at:

- local residents
- day visitors from outside the area
- domestic tourists

- foreign tourists
- school parties

ACTIVITY

Using a selection of leaflets and brochures for tourist attractions and holidays, identify the different segments that are being targeted. Share the information within your group. C

ACTIVITY

As a group, imagine you have been asked to create a new toy for 3–5 year olds. Interview some parents of young children, local nurseries etc., to find out if there is a gap in the market. Choose the type of toy and a name for it, and then design the advertising materials and packaging. Suggest a suitable price, bearing in mind competing products, and where you would choose to place your advertisements. C N

The 'marketing mix' and 'the four Ps'

This activity would involve your group in the 'marketing mix' simplified as 'the four Ps' in marketing jargon (see Table 16 on page 68). These are:

- Product
- Price
- Place
- Promotion

ACTIVITY

YOU'LL HAVE TO DRIVE A LONG WAY TO BEAT THIS OFFER

At the Burstin, group organisers enjoy competitive rates, and now with inclusive National Express travel to the Hotel, no group is too small! You and your group have all the facilities of the UK's leading leisure hotel at your fingertips! Dial 01303 854500 now!!

BIG DEAL

SPECTACULAR LIVE CABARET AND DANCING EVERY NIGHT
★ ★ ★ ★
INDOOR SWIMMING POOL, SAUNA, FITNESS ROOM & SNOOKER
★ ★ ★ ★
STAR CABARETS AND FUN WEEKENDS
★ ★ ★ ★
THREE BARS, BISTRO AND RESTAURANTS
★ ★ ★ ★
FREE DAY TRIPS TO FRANCE
★ ★ ★ ★
EN-SUITE ACCOMMODATION
★ ★ ★ ★
FABULOUS DISCOUNTS AT LOCAL ATTRACTIONS AVAILABLE
★ ★ ★ ★
GROUP TRAVEL OPTIONS AVAILABLE

XMAS, MILLENNIUM & NEW YEAR ALTERNATIVE AVAILABLE NOW FROM £120

Call 01303 854500 for our brochure and competitive group rates now.
Hotel Burstin, The Harbour, Folkestone, Kent CT20 1TX

Advert for Burstin Hotel

This advertisement for the Burstin Hotel was aimed at group organisers. Identify the different services provided for:

- **members of a tour group**

- **group organisers**

- **individual hotel guests**

PRODUCT

As stated earlier, the 'product' will often be intangible, i.e. you cannot see it – a holiday, for example, or a course of golf lessons. It is only after the customer has bought the product that they can try it out. Selling holidays has been described as 'selling dreams' because the customer has to rely on a brochure and discussion with a travel agent or tour operator to make a decision to buy. Even with the use of technology and the ability to view a resort on video, or through the use of a multi media computer, it is still only possible to judge a holiday location by actually going there and trying it out. Even personal recommendations are not foolproof, as everyone has a

Most people's idea of a holiday!

different idea of what makes a holiday enjoyable for them.

Service products have many different parts, all of which contribute to the experience offered to the customer. For example, when selling someone a ticket to visit a tourist attraction, an agent will be offering:

- Entrance to the attraction.
- Accessibility to all the facilities – rides, exhibits, catering, toilets.
- A type of environment – lively, peaceful, safe, exciting.
- Delivery of service by qualified staff – guides, ride operators, caterers, first aid assistants.
- An identity or 'brand' that is recognisable, e.g. Disneyland, Alton Towers or Center Parcs.

Product design will be aided by the results of market research, and various brand names will be tried on the public before the final name is chosen. There are also other considerations when choosing brand names. For instance, they must be inoffensive and they must not already be registered by another company. If products are to be exported then care has to be taken over the name and colour of packaging, because some names and colours could be offensive or just unattractive to foreigners.

After sales service

When providing a product or service, it is extremely important to consider the type and level of after sales service that will be needed. Customers are used to buying products that

	HOTEL	SCHEDULED AIRLINE	MUSEUM
Product Designed characteristics/ packaging	Location/building size/ grounds/design/room size/facilities in hotel furnishings/décor/ lighting/catering styles.	Routes/service frequency. Aircraft type/size. Seat size/ space. Décor, meals, style.	Building size/design/facilities. Types of collection. Size of collection. Interior display/interpretation.
Service component	Staff numbers/ uniforms/attitudes.	Staff numbers, uniforms/attitudes.	Staff numbers, uniforms/attitudes.
Branding	e.g. Holiday Inn, Savoy, Meridien.	e.g. American Airlines, British Airways, Virgin Atlantic.	e.g. Tate Gallery (London) Metropolitan Museum (New York).
Image/reputation/ positioning	e.g. upmarket, downmarket.	e.g. reliable, exotic food, badly-managed.	e.g. dull, exciting, modern.
Price Normal or regular price. Promotional price (for each product offered)	Rack rates. Corporate rates. Privileged user rates. Tour operator discount rate.	First class/business/ tourist fares. APEX. Standby. Charter. Consolidated fares.	(assuming charge made) Adult rate, senior citizen rate. Group/party rates. Children rate. Friends of the museum rate.
Promotion (solo and collaborative) Advertising (TV/ radio/press/journals) Sales promotion/ merchandising Public relations Brochure production and distribution Sales force	Examples not provided, since these are generally self-evident and specific to individual organisations.		
Place Channels of distribution including reservation systems	Computerised reservation systems (CRS). Other hotels in group. Travel agents. Tour operators. Airlines. 800 telephone lines.	Computerised reservation systems (CRS). City offices. Airport desks. Travel agents. Other airlines. 800 telephone lines.	Other museums. Tourist information offices. Hotel desks. Schools/colleges.

TABLE 16 *Examples of the marketing mix*

Source: Marketing Travel and Tourism, *Victor T. C. Middleton, Butterworth Heinemann*

are covered by some sort of guarantee by the manufacturer, and also consumer laws which ensure that goods are sold 'fit for purpose'. For example, electrical goods must work and work safely and shoes should not fall apart the first time they are worn. It is, however, much more difficult to ensure that a service will meet these expectations. A customer cannot take a holiday back, for example, as he could with a tangible product. Therefore, any company offering services has to consider what they will do if things go wrong. This will form part of the marketing and promotion strategy and has to be decided at an early stage.

The most easily recognisable offer of after sales service in leisure and tourism is found in the section of a holiday brochure covering booking conditions. Some companies call this section a 'Fair Trading Charter', and it sets out the responsibilities of the customer and the tour operator, including the steps to take in the event of a complaint (dealing with complaints will be covered in the next chapter).

ACTIVITY

1. **Compare several different types of holiday brochures and how they offer after sales service. If possible, compare major operators with smaller independent type companies.** **C**

2. **Discuss other types of after sales service that leisure and tourism organisations offer their customers.** **C**

PRICING

Deciding on the price of a product is very difficult. Companies need to make a profit, but at the same time they need to know what the public will be prepared to pay and also what the competitors' prices are like. There is fierce competition in the travel business, where profit margins have been cut drastically by the major companies in order to become the largest operators. Airlines, ferry companies, car hire companies, all have to keep their prices at a competitive level. Ferry companies in particular have had to lower their fares to compete with the Channel Tunnel, especially in the winter months.

Some prices are determined by outside factors, such as legislation governing fare increases or the need to make seasonal changes to cope with different levels of demand. Not all leisure and tourism products will be priced to make a profit, though. Many prices will be set at a level which are only sufficient to cover the costs of providing the service. For example, many leisure activities are not run to make a profit, such as youth clubs, amateur dramatics groups or other similar organisations, or they may be subsidised by the local authority, such as a museum or a leisure centre.

Church buildings are often used for leisure activities and non-church organisations pay a small fee for the hire of the buildings. Some leisure and tourism facilities are shared between private and public ownership. For example, a community centre owned by the local council may be used by a variety of voluntary organisations: playgroup, mother and baby club, scouts and guides, and youth club. Other users, such as privately-run dance, aerobic and yoga classes, will pay the council for the hire of the centre. School halls and sports

PROFIT-MAKING ACTIVITIES	NON-PROFIT-MAKING ACTIVITIES	ACTIVITIES SHARED BETWEEN PROFIT-MAKING AND NON-PROFIT-MAKING ORGANISATIONS
Accommodation and catering	Youth clubs, drama groups	Non-vocational educational classes, e.g. crafts, yoga, music
Holidays, tours, excursions	Youth hostels	Private dance classes in a school hall
Theme parks, zoos, tourist attractions	Libraries, museums, art galleries	Car boot sale in church car park

TABLE 17 *Types of activities*

facilities are often opened to the public at weekends and during school holidays, providing income either for the school or the local authority.

ACTIVITY

Find out what activities take place in your local community centre and whether they are for profit. Does your school or college hire out rooms, sports facilities etc? Ⓒ

Prices also have to be set at the right level to provide value for money and encourage repeat business. Some prices have to cover agents' commission or leave sufficient margin to allow for a discount at a later date.

When considering the price of a product or service, it is sometimes necessary to consider whether to allow for payment over a period of time. To a certain extent, this is what happens when a customer buys a holiday. The customer pays a deposit, but doesn't have to pay the full price until nearer the date of departure. Sometimes a customer is allowed credit and actually has the benefit of the service before paying in full. Other examples of this would be a course of swimming lessons, membership of a leisure club or a holiday.

PLACE

The term 'place' in leisure and tourism is rather confusing. In marketing it usually means where the product is sold, but there is a dual meaning in leisure and tourism as it can mean both the product **and** where it is sold. An example of this would be a product such as Alton Towers Theme Park in Staffordshire, which would be sold in many 'places': travel agencies, tour operators, coach companies, schools etc. Package holidays are another typical example of the dual meaning of place in leisure and tourism, as the holidays can be sold through a travel agency, over the telephone, via the Internet.

'Place' also relates to the positioning of information and display material. Leisure and tourism operators produce many different types of display materials: brochures, leaflets, posters, showcards, videos, films, etc. These operators use specialist companies (merchandisers) to ensure that their products are displayed in the most prominent position in travel agencies, tourist information centres, at airports, bus and rail stations or in hotels, for example. This also ensures that displays are regularly updated and new supplies are ordered.

These displays are referred to as 'point-of-sale material'. Clearly, each supplier of point-of-sale material wants their product to be displayed in the most prominent position, and this can cause problems where there are many similar products on offer, for example in a tourist information centre or a travel agency. Sales representatives visit these outlets regularly to ensure that their promotional display is being placed in the best position, as well as to keep staff updated on any new developments.

The distribution of this material is extremely important. There is a great deal of wastage of printed matter in this industry and this is extremely expensive. There are also increasing environmental concerns about the unnecessary amount of litter created by the over production of such promotional materials. Tour operators will distribute their brochures to agents on the basis of previous sales, so that unproductive agents will perhaps only receive a file copy.

For many years, the public have been able to seek out bargain holidays through the use of teletext. This provided the information, but entailed a telephone booking. New technology has now been developed which will enable customers to book through their televisions without a telephone if they do not have access to the Internet, which has had a phenomenal rise of popularity, with new sites opening up daily offering late deals, cut price holidays, etc. Books and compact discs and many other leisure goods, such as computer games, are offered for sale at much lower prices than in the High Street stores and this has resulted in a boom in direct sales. Many leisure goods can now be bought this way.

One airline, easyJet, will only sell tickets through the Internet from 2000. Other holiday companies are able to offer last minute bargains right up to the time of departure, through this method of advertising.

---

easyJet sells a record 66% of all seats online!

easyJet's latest Internet sale, which closed at midnight last night, has been a phenomenal success. During the seven days between 17–23 November, easyJet sold 92,636 seats online, representing 66% of all seat sales.

This fantastic performance smashes easyJet's own existing record of 60%, which was achieved during an Internet sale run in early October.

Once again, easyJet has achieved another world record in the aviation industry, as no other airline comes close to selling this proportion of seats online.

easyJet press release, 24 November 1999

PROMOTION

Promotion includes all the activities used to raise the public's awareness of products and create a demand. Typical activities include:

- merchandising
- advertising
- sales promotions
- brochure production
- public relations

ACTIVITY

Prepare a chart similar to the one in Table 16 (see page 68) for a tour operator, car ferry operator and a theme park, using a word processor if possible. Ⓒ ⒤ⓣ

Promotion Methods
Merchandising

Merchandising is the term used to describe all the marketing activities that are used to raise the customer's interest in a product or service, other than through conventional types of advertising or through the use of public relations. These activities include:

- demonstrations
- special displays
- free samples
- personal selling

In the highly competitive leisure and tourism market, many innovative ways of presenting products to the customer have been created. Amongst the most popular are the many exhibitions aimed at the public, such as holiday shows, boat shows, camping and caravanning shows. Displays of winter sports equipment at ski shows also provide an opportunity to try the sport on artificial slopes.

There are also trade exhibitions, such as the World Travel Market, and regional shows where tourist attractions are able to present themselves to travel organisers. The leisure industry has many trade shows where the wide-ranging equipment used in such places as gyms, fairgrounds, and theme parks are on display.

There are many special offers used to entice customers to buy a product. Sometimes customers are offered linking products, such as free travel insurance if you book a holiday or free golf club membership for one month when you buy a set of golf clubs. Vouchers or coupons offering free 'taster' days at a gym, or money off membership fees for a limited period, are a popular way of introducing new members. Free entrance into competitions when purchasing a product is another way of increasing sales.

ACTIVITY

Compile a dossier of different merchandising examples that you have seen in your area. Share them with the rest of your group and discuss how effective you think they were. Did they interest you in the product? Would you have looked for the product without seeing the promotion? Ⓒ 💬

The term 'merchandising' is also used to cover products that are sold using the logos from another product. For example, pens and schoolbags, with a football team's logo on. This is an important source of income for the football team (who get a fee) as well as the pen and bag manufacturers. This should not, however, be confused with sponsorship.

Advertising

Advertisements are a well known aspect of promotion. It is difficult to escape seeing some form of advertising every day. They are used to draw the public's attention to new products, or to remind them of the existence of well established products. There are many

GARDEN FETE
IN AID OF COUNTY AIR AMBULANCE
At 2 Morgan Close
(off Alcaster Road) Studley,
on Saturday 24th
10am – 4pm
Admission 50p inc.
drink/cake
PLANTS – CAKES –
BRIC-A-BRAC – TOMBOLA
and many other stalls

Visit
Henley-in-Arden
MARKET & CAR BOOT
Wednesday
Saturday
Sunday
8am – 2pm
Tel: 01564 792154
Evenings: 01789 721028

Top Note Fairs
Antique & Collectors Fair
CRAWFORD HALL,
BIDFORD-ON-AVON
24th–25th July 10–5
Refreshments, Free car park

THIS IS THE
BIG ONE
STRATFORD'S MOST POPULAR
CAR BOOT SALE
EVERY SATURDAY AT CATTLE
MARKET. £6.00 PER CAR
01789 292898

**SUNDAY 17th JULY
RECORD FAIR.** Motorcycle
Museum (Nr. NEC). All types,
9.30–4pm. Entry £2.50. £1
afternoon.

July 23rd
GRIEG CENTRE DISCO Alcester.
Over 18's only. 10pm till 1am.
01789 400073

Examples of local activity advertising   *Source:* Why! Magazine

possible locations for advertising:

- Newspapers, magazines, and leaflets
- Television and radio
- Cinemas
- Hoardings
- Buses, taxis, trains
- On the Internet, Ceefax, Oracle

Advertisements are used to persuade people to do something, usually to buy a new or existing product, but sometimes to draw attention to a change in a product such as 'different shaped bottle' or 'now even more rides included in the price'. Advertising is also used to attract people to an event, to provide information, or to recruit staff.

 ACTIVITY

List as many advertisements as you can remember in five minutes and then put them into the locations given opposite. Which type of advertisement did you remember best? Can you remember exactly what was being sold? Share this information with a partner and see if you remember the same advertisements, or different ones. Discuss whether you would consider buying the products advertised. **C**

Source: Group Travel Organiser Magazine

 ACTIVITY

Look at the advertisement above. Who is the 'target'? What is the purpose of the advertisement, and why has the company placed it in Group Travel Magazine? Discuss other suitable publications for advertising this venue.

Even well-established companies need to advertise to retain customer loyalty, repeat business and their share of the market. Fierce competition makes it necessary to advertise. Consider the amount of advertising for holidays in the winter months. If one company starts an advertising campaign, all the other tour operators and travel agencies also start to advertise. Advertising toys at Christmas time is another example.

A change of house style, address, pricing policy or company name will be advertised to past, present and future customers.

Advertising is essential to attract new customers. For instance, a company with a rather old fashioned reputation may decide to update its image and want to attract a younger type of customer, so it will use different advertising methods or place advertisements in different magazines for the youth market.

Companies who have lost customers need to advertise to retrieve them from the competition.

Most advertising is paid for by the organisation whose products are being advertised. Occasionally advertisements are sponsored. For example, local companies may all contribute to the advertising costs for a charity event by advertising in the programme.

Sometimes public services in leisure and tourism will advertise. This is usually to provide information to the public, such as changes to passport and visa regulations, customs regulations, health warnings. Codes of practice are also advertised by public bodies such as HM Customs Service.

The types of advertisements chosen by companies are usually determined by the budget available. Charity event organisers are likely to place small advertisements in local papers, shop windows, schools and on posters

Lacoste advertisement

Source: Lacoste

near to the event, whereas large sportswear manufacturers can afford to place their advertisements on television, in cinemas, on hoardings at sports events and in cities, and in the press. Small advertisements in shops, supermarkets, newsagents and local newspapers are a popular way for charities to advertise events as they are very cheap and sometimes even free.

 **ACTIVITY**

1. Using local newspapers, leaflets and magazines, find an example of each of the following leisure and tourism advertisements:

- **for an existing product or service**
- **a public service advertisement**
- **announcing an event**
- **introducing a new product**
- **announcing a change in pricing**

2. Compare your findings with the rest of your group and complete a dossier of advertisements for your area. Index the types of advertisements by type of advertiser. (Public, or voluntary or private).

The careful selection of media is an essential part of advertising. Traditionally these are:

- press
- radio
- television
- cinema
- outdoor (posters and transport) and, more recently,
- the Internet

Other means of advertising include:

- sponsorship
- calendars
- direct mail leaflets
- matchboxes
- free gifts such as pens, desk items, diaries
- free samples
- point of sale materials (show cards, posters, year planners)
- names on hot air balloons
- banners at events

Large companies will usually employ an advertising agency to handle all their promotional work, but smaller companies and voluntary organisations usually have to handle their own.

ACTIVITY

Prepare a leaflet for a local event – real or imaginary – preferably using a word processor, and decide how you will distribute it. Also, draft out and record a short radio commercial for one of the following:

- **A charity football match**

- **A 'taster' day at the local leisure centre**

- **A new air route from your nearest airport**

- **The opening of a restaurant**

You should ensure that you include all the relevant details:

- **date, time, place**

- **cost**

- **booking arrangements**

- **address and telephone numbers**

Direct marketing

This is an increasingly popular way of promoting leisure and tourism products.

As shown in Table 18, there are many direct marketing methods used in leisure and tourism.

ACTIVITY

Collect examples of direct marketing and categorise them as shown in Table 18.

Direct mail	• to previous customers • to purchased lists of targeted prospects • via lists owned by third parties • in response to enquiries • via joint mailing with relevant partners
Telephone/ tele-marketing	• to targeted customer lists • in response to enquiries
Door-to-door distribution	• to targeted blocks of residential streets/roads
Travel-related exhibitions	• to enquirers at stands; e.g. boat shows, travel exhibitions, and caravan and camping shows
Media advertising	• with coupons • with response telephone numbers, or 0800 lines
Interactive TV	• on line TV terminals in customers' homes, used to make bookings direct

TABLE 18 *Direct response marketing methods to reach individual consumers of travel*

Source: Marketing in Travel and Tourism, *Victor T.C. Middleton, Heinemann*

Public relations

There are companies and individual consultants specialising in public relations. They are responsible for dealing with the media on behalf of their clients and will arrange advertising and other activities to promote their clients' goods and services. They may also be asked to represent their clients in public. For example, if there is an accident, or reports criticising the company in the press, the public relations company will often make statements on behalf of their clients to the media. They will also advise a company on its image with the public, and if something is badly affecting that image, such as complaints or scandals.

A public relations consultant will be responsible for drafting press releases to advise the public on new products or services, staff changes, staff achievements, such as 'best sales consultant', future plans etc. By presenting a good press release, the company should receive useful (free) editorial, which is usually received very well by the public, who trust an editorial more than an advertisement. The public is more wary of advertisements since they know they have been paid for by the advertiser (see the later section on press releases).

Special events, such as product launches, educational visits, exhibitions, demonstrations, conferences, lunches and dinners, are usually arranged by public relations consultants either within the company or from outside the company being promoted.

Personal selling

This is still an important aspect of promotion in leisure and tourism. Well trained, knowledgeable sales staff are still valued by customers who will often use a seemingly old-fashioned business, such as a travel agency, in order to get personal service from staff who know them and their tastes well. A good sales person will always try to match the customer's needs, as you will see in Chapter 5 on Customer Service.

Staff who will be involved in face-to-face selling in leisure and tourism are:

- travel agents
- resort representatives selling excursions
- cabin crew selling duty free goods
- leisure centre staff selling coaching, sports equipment
- timeshare sales staff
- ticket sales people in theatres, theme parks, tourist attractions
- catering and accommodation staff

Displays

The most obvious use of display in leisure and tourism is the posters and display cards (called point-of-sale material) in travel agencies, tourist information centres and outside theatres and cinemas. Other displays are in shop windows and at exhibitions or in shopping centres. Large displays will often be placed in public areas, for example at an airport. These displays are usually to announce a new product and will be displayed for a limited time. It is important that the display is always kept clean and fresh and is not allowed to get damaged.

ACTIVITY

Prepare two items of point-of-sale material for use in a leisure organisation. One item should be prepared using a word processor.

Sponsorship in the leisure and tourism industry

Source: Action-Plus/Glyn Kirk

Sponsorship

Sponsorship takes many forms, from a small company sponsoring the local boys football team to the large sponsorship found in motor racing or round the world yacht racing. What exactly is sponsorship? Broadly speaking, it is when a company agrees to fund an activity in exchange for which it gets publicity. Most often the publicity is obvious, as for example in the case of a football team, having its sponsor's name prominently printed on their shirts; but sometimes a company will be more discreet and will simply be acknowledged in a programme.

For example, it is common for large organisations such as banks to sponsor musical concerts. In this case, the programme for the concert will reflect this. Many major leisure and tourism events are sponsored.

Sponsorship of an individual sports person is also common, and many of our finest athletes could not participate at high levels of competition without the financial support of their sponsors.

 **ACTIVITY**

Using local and national newspapers, identify examples of sports personalities and their sponsors, and events that have been sponsored.

Demonstrations and visits

As mentioned previously, leisure and tourism products and services are mostly intangible and, therefore, it is difficult for the public to try something before they buy it. Leisure centres, golf clubs and tennis clubs hold open days so that the public can try out different activities before committing themselves to joining. Exhibitions enable the public to try out sports and leisure equipment or taste the food of a particular country. Timeshare and overseas property companies invite potential buyers to view the accommodation, often providing transport and hotel accommodation to the resort. Travel agents are invited on educational visits to sample new resorts, new forms of transport, or familiarise themselves with an area. These visits are called 'familiarisation trips' and are highly valued by staff working in travel and tourism.

ACTIVITY

1. **Prepare a two day familiarisation trip to a place of your choice, suitable for trainee travel agents.** **C**

2. **Choose a piece of gym or sports equipment and demonstrate it to your class.** **C**

Promotions

Many types of promotions are used in leisure and tourism They include:

- 'Two for the price of one' offers
- Vouchers for money off or free entrance
- Special discounts
- Price reductions
- Free gifts
- Prize draws
- Loyalty schemes

Advertisers can easily compile an address list from the names on competition entries or special offer application forms which can later be used as a mailing list. Holidays and luxury goods, such as the latest TV and audio equipment, and cars, are the most popular prizes.

There have been increased numbers of loyalty schemes. These usually operate by the customer of a particular store or service using a special member's card, which is allocated points when the customer makes a purchase.

These points can be exchanged for a variety of leisure and tourism products such as books, compact discs, discounts on holidays and ferry crossings or holidays. Air Miles is one of the most popular of these schemes, as customers of airlines, supermarkets and other retail outlets, and a wide variety of other services can collect the air miles towards the purchase of air tickets. The scheme has been extended to enable air miles members to use their Air Miles for entrance to theme parks, cinemas etc.

ACTIVITY

As a group, gather a dossier of examples of all the above types of promotional techniques. Your dossier should reflect a wide range of leisure and tourism products and services, nationally and locally, including public, private and voluntary organisations, small companies and large national and international companies. **C**

Promotion material used in leisure and tourism

Your dossier from the previous activity should include examples of all the materials used in promotional work.

1. BROCHURES AND LEAFLETS

You need to examine different types of brochures. The most commonly used leisure and tourism brochures will be those for holidays. These are expensive to produce and distribute, but they are an essential selling

COLLECTING

Collecting's *a breeze*

25 bonus miles on sailings to France

Pick up **25 bonus AIR MILES** when you take a 5-day break to France from Portsmouth this Summer. Travel to Le Havre in style on a 5 star Cruiseferry. Alternatively travel to Cherbourg by ferry or 'fly' across in just 2 hours 45 minutes by SuperStar Express.

Fares are from £95 for a car and up to 5 passengers for a 5-day return. Travel out on an afternoon sailing and back on a morning sailing.

You'll also pick up **1 mile for every £2 spent** on tickets of £30 or over.

This offer cannot be combined with any other offer. Bookings must be made at least 14 days in advance. Full payment is required at the time of booking. Travel must be completed (both outward and return) between 15/6/99 and 30/11/99. Bookings made through the AIR MILES Holiday Hotline are not eligible for this offer. Travelling on different sailings will incur a supplement. High season bookings and SuperStar Express bookings will incur a supplement of £10 per vehicle, per single leg . Accommodation will be charged for at full brochure price . Bonus miles will be allocated as soon as possible after travel is completed. Space is subject to availability. Normal Terms and Conditions apply.

P&O PORTSMOUTH
INTERNET: http://www.poportsmouth.com

BONUS OFFER
25 bonus miles on sailings to France.

OFFER
1 mile per £2 spent on tickets of £30 or over.

Call **0870 2424 999**

and quote 'Portsmouth Miles' offer.

25 bonus miles on breaks in France

Pick up **25 bonus AIR MILES** when you take a Summer break of up to 6 days in France. Travel on our exciting Super ferries to Calais and relax ready for your break. Fares for this stay begin from just £119 for a car and up to 9 passengers.

You'll also earn **1 mile for every £2 spent** on tickets of £30 or more.

Note: A £10 supplement will be charged for outward travel on a Friday or Saturday. A £25 supplement will be charged for minibuses, motorhomes and vehicles designed for commercial use in excess of 1.83m high and no longer than 6.00m when travelling on a non commercial journey. Trailers will be charged at the standard rates current at the time of booking. This offer cannot be combined with any other offer. Travel must be completed (both outward and return) between 15/6/99 and 30/9/99. No refunds or amendments are permitted. Bookings made through the AIR MILES Holiday Hotline are not eligible for this offer. Bonus miles will be allocated as soon as possible after travel is completed. Other Terms and Conditions are shown in the P&O Stena Line Ferry Guide '99. The offer is subject to restricted space and sailings.

P&O Stena LINE

BONUS OFFER
25 bonus miles on breaks in France.

OFFER
1 mile per £2 spent on tickets of £30 or over.

Call **087 0600 0600**

and quote 'Dover Miles' to book. Or visit your local travel agent.

28 COLLECTING

Ways to collect air miles

Source: AIR MILES Travel Promotions Ltd.

tool for tour operators. When examining brochures you will find that they include:

- Introductory pages, describing the company and its special strategies;
- Special discounts and features for children, senior citizens and groups;
- General resort information (country, specific region, then actual resort);
- Regional and resort maps;
- Detailed accommodation information;
- Price grids;
- Transport arrangements (flights, transfers, travel times);
- Holiday insurance;
- Booking conditions, 'fair booking charters' or similar promises of guaranteed customer satisfaction.

Most brochures are produced in colour on good quality paper, with excellent photography. As this is the first opportunity to attract a customer, a brochure has to be visually appealing. A glance at any travel agency brochure rack will demonstrate the amount of competition there is, and the tour operators have to ensure that their brochure is the most eye-catching.

As well as being a powerful promotional tool, brochures have to comply with various consumer protection codes and regulations, such as the EC Package Holiday Directive, Trades Description Act, Sale of Goods Act, Misrepresentation Act.

Leaflets are used to describe all types of leisure facilities and tourist attractions, and can be used in a variety of ways. They are posted directly to members, as for instance in the case of the Ronnie Scott's Jazz Club (see

ACTIVITY

Compare the front page of Sky Tours' Brochure for 1957 on page 82 with a current Thomsons Holiday brochure. (Thomson Holidays bought Sky Tours).

The Sky Tours brochure was A5 size, printed on low quality paper with poor colour. Now look at the layout on the page and compare this with the current brochure. What do you notice has changed? What are the reasons for these changes? Ⓒ

example on page 83), and they are distributed in tourist information centres, other distribution points, and inside newspapers as well as at the actual attraction itself. Leaflets are generally cheaper to produce and can be changed more frequently than a large brochure.

Apart from effective design, the brochure has to be distributed to the targeted customers. Possible distribution points have to be researched and these could include agents, community centres, libraries, exhibitions, tourist attractions, town halls, and so on. Distribution research plays an important part in the planning of promotional activities.

ACTIVITY

Examine the information on page 83 about Ronnie Scott's Club. List all the different purposes served by this leaflet. Refer back to the reasons why companies advertise. Ⓒ

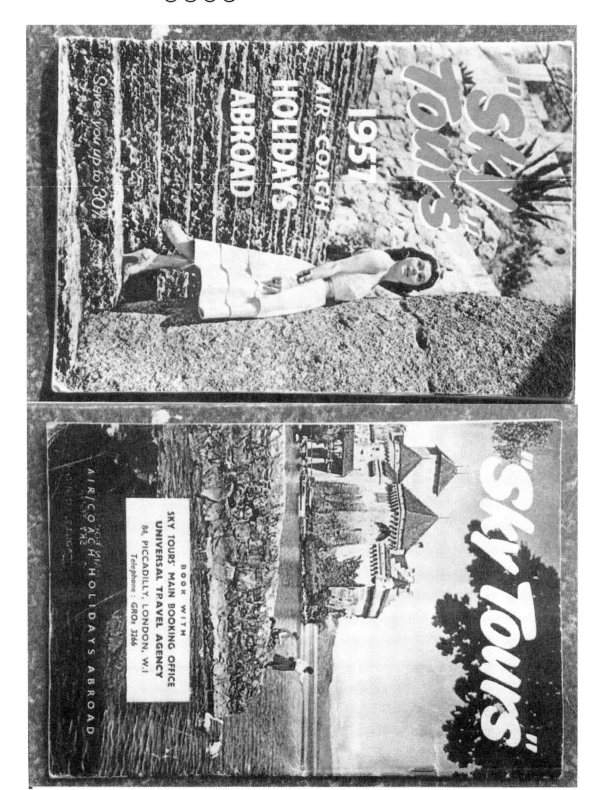

'Sky Tours' brochure advertising holidays abroad

Leaflet for Ronnie Scott's club

Tour operators sell their holidays through travel agents or by direct sales through the post and over the telephone. Both methods need the tour operator's brochure. The distribution research the operator will carry out will use information already gained relating to past sales performances of the different travel agents. In order to minimise waste, the numbers of brochures distributed to each agent will usually be in proportion to the number of previous bookings from that agent. The only means of judging how effective the brochure distribution method has been, will be the numbers of bookings received as a result.

Leaflet distribution is even more difficult to assess, as visitors to attractions may or may not have seen a leaflet first. Many leaflets are wasted because they have been placed in the wrong locations, for example large numbers of leaflets about a small tourist attraction in Cornwall being placed in a library in Yorkshire is very unlikely to bring new customers unless they were already planning to go to Cornwall.

2. POSTERS AND OTHER POINT-OF-SALE ITEMS

Posters for leisure and tourism have been produced for over 100 years. The early posters advertised rail journeys as shown here.

Posters are placed on hoardings in urban areas, on public transport, in railway and underground entrances, and inside travel agencies, tourist information centres and entertainment venues such as theatres and exhibition centres. It is difficult to assess the effectiveness of posters alone, since they are often used in conjunction with other forms of promotion.

3. MERCHANDISING MATERIALS

The commonest forms of these materials are pens, pencils and other desk items such as notepads, clocks, calculators, diaries and calendars. They are handed out to potential customers or people who could influence potential customers, e.g. a travel agency's open/closed sign with the logo of a travel principal, such as a ferry operator, will be seen regularly by staff and customers alike.

Staff coffee mugs advertising sportswear are a constant reminder to sales staff of that company's name. Visitors to leisure and tourism exhibitions and trade fairs are likely to come away with many such souvenirs. Special events, such as carnivals, are a good opportunity for leisure and tourism

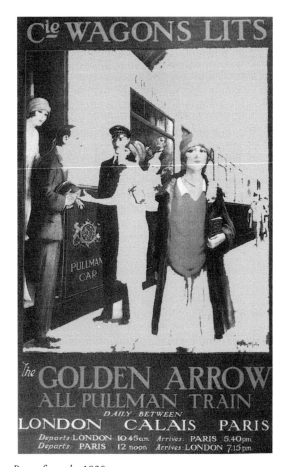

Poster from the 1920s

companies to advertise using balloons – small ones or hot air ones – and travel bags, and T-shirts carrying company logos are popular prizes in competitions and prize draws. (If you are organising a fund-raising event it is often possible to get some of these items from leisure and tourism organisations and companies to use as raffle prizes.)

Sportswear carrying a team's logo is one of the commonest examples of merchandising. Famous football teams even merchandise such items as bed linen, lampshades and mirrors – all of which raise the profile of the club concerned and also raise money.

4. VIDEOS

Videos are useful promotional tools. They can give a customer an insight into a destination, be used as a training aid (in, for example, aerobics) or be used to demonstrate new products such as sport and leisure equipment. Sales representatives can take them to the customer or retailer for demonstration purposes and customers can borrow them to look at with the whole family. This is especially useful if a holiday is being chosen as there are now many holiday destination videos available.

5. PRESS RELEASES

As mentioned earlier, it is the role of a public relations consultant to prepare regular press releases. These are then sent to the media in the hope that they will be used. As press releases are not paid advertisements, it is important that they are sent to the appropriate media, at the right time, i.e. allowing time for the editor to include it in a publication. They have to attract the editor's attention and create interest.

Press releases need to be very carefully written and presented, on special letter headings, giving the name and address of the public relations company, and 24 hour contact numbers. If the release is cleverly worded, it is likely to be printed without alteration. The copy should be double spaced with wide margins. The opening sentence must immediately attract attention and convey the message. This could be an announcement of a new product, destination, change of staff, change of company name or to draw attention to the fact that a well-known personality has used a particular company's service.

Local newspapers are usually very receptive to press releases about local events, so smaller organisations and voluntary groups often gain publicity in this way. This is called 'free' publicity – even though larger firms will usually employ a consultant to draw up the release.

Press releases can be sent to general media or to the media for the specific trade. For instance, a press release about a new golf and leisure development would be sent to all golf publications, as well as magazines such as *Leisure Management.* and quality Sunday newspaper magazines. Press releases are used to notify the media about forthcoming events, for example the appearance of a celebrity to open the event.

Unlike paid advertising, which can be booked for a particular date, press releases are slightly risky in that it depends on the other news which a newspaper or television news editor wants to print at a particular time, so there is no guarantee that anything will be printed at all.

ACTIVITY

If you are involved in arranging an event, prepare a press release and send it to the local radio, newspapers and television centre. Remember to make it very eye-catching, and original. Editors have to read many boring releases! Ⓒ ⒾⓉ

An area might gain free publicity when it becomes newsworthy because of its residents, such as when royalty, film stars etc. move into the area, or because it is featured in a film, book or television series. The

TV and Movies

With its fine scenery, rolling countryside, secluded rural villages, historic towns and cities, it is little wonder that so many TV series and movies have been filmed in locations around Yorkshire. Current classics such as 'Brideshead Revisited', 'Emmerdale', 'Heartbeat' and 'Last of the Summer Wine' continue to draw millions of viewers to the TV screen whilst blockbuster movies such as 'Robin Hood, Prince of Thieves', 'Memphis Belle' and 'Secret Garden' have all used Yorkshire locations as inspirational backdrops for some of the most famous actors and actresses in the world. Bring your cameras and capture your own films for posterity!

Coastal Surprises

MORNING:

Robin Hood's Bay
One of Yorkshire's well known coastal resorts has been used as the evocative setting for 'Carrington', the true story of the dazzling but doomed English painter Dora Carrington and her unconventional relationship with the eminent writer Lytton Strachey. Jonathan Pryce recently scooped the Evening Standard Best Actor award for his portrayal of Strachey.
Robin Hood's Bay offered the TV film crew two locations in one - to the north they had the perfect setting for the rugged Welsh coast and to the south they had the scene "on the Sussex Downs" where, against the distant roar of heavy gun fire across the channel, Lytton first tries to kiss Dora.
In times gone by the Bay was also the location for BBC's film version of Charles Dicken's 'David Copperfield'. As well as enjoying the sights and sounds of the coast, why not pay a visit to the Music in Miniature Exhibition, ☎ (01947) 880512 or the Ravenscar Coastal Centre which is 5 mins drive towards Scarborough, ☎ (01723) 870138 & 870423.

TV Town Itineraries

Yorkshire's many vibrant towns have played host to many well known films and TV series, some of which are listed below. As such, we recommend that you consider creating specific TV Town itineraries which combine the best of actual filming locations and good value Yorkshire shopping. Please contact the Yorkshire Tourist Board if you are interested in receiving additional help on (01904) 707961.

Harrogate - Stay Lucky, Ain't Misbehavin', Chariots of Fire
Leeds - Harry's Game, Jimmy's, The Good Old Days, A Touch of Frost
Bradford - Band of Gold, Billy Liar
Halifax - A Great Day Out!, In Loving Memory
Barnsley - Kes
Grimsby - Memphis Belle
Hull - Only Fools & Horses
Doncaster - Open All Hours, PC Penrose
Wakefield - This Sporting Life, The Beiderbecke Affair
Sheffield - The Full Monty

TV Treasures!

Many of Yorkshire's fine historic houses have been the setting for TV series and movies. There is a separate itinerary section for historic houses in this brochure, but to whet your appetite perhaps these names may jog your memory?
Castle Howard -   Brideshead Revisited
Fountains Abbey - The Final Conflict
Lotherton Hall -   Sherlock Holmes, Darling Buds of May
Allerton Park -   The Secret Garden
Broughton Hall -   Woman of Substance

Heartbeat
Heartbeat Holidays offer the only official packages for groups based on this hugely popular TV series. Your group can enjoy the rolling Yorkshire countryside on board the North Yorkshire Moors Railway and visit the Aidensfield Arms and the surgery in Goathland. (Accommodation is in the Blackwell Grange, Darlington).
North Yorkshire Moors Railway, Pickering Station, North Yorkshire YO18 7AJ ☎ (01751) 477433

Emmerdale
For a truly Yorkshire day out, visit the secluded village of Esholt (known as Beckindale to millions of avid TV viewers) and have a pint in the Woolpack! Complement this with the stunning countryside and close-by market town of Otley, and you have a recipe for success!

Example of free publicity for tourism areas

Source: Yorkshire Tourist Board

tourism industry makes full use of such information by promoting the area to fans. Overseas visitors as well as UK residents are very interested in seeing how the royals live, and when Buckingham Palace was opened to the public it was soon fully booked. Stratford upon Avon became famous as a tourist venue over a hundred years ago, when scholars came to visit the home of Shakespeare. Now it is an essential visit for overseas visitors touring the UK. 'Last of the Summer Wine', 'Heartbeat' and 'Emmerdale Farm' have placed Yorkshire firmly on the tourist map. Readers of Catherine Cookson's books make pilgrimages to her home town of South Shields which is now promoted as 'Catherine Cookson Country'.

ACTIVITY

Research an area that has become well-known through a film, television programme or because of its connections with someone famous. Compile a dossier of the ways in which this is exploited by the local tourism industry. (C)

Promotional campaigns in leisure and tourism

The success of promotional campaigns depends on thorough planning beforehand. Whether the organisation is large or small, the basic stages will remain the same. Larger leisure and tourism organisations, such as travel companies, hotel groups, airlines and sports clubs will usually engage specialists to carry out these activities on their behalf if they do not have their own marketing department. Smaller organisations, such as voluntary clubs, will have to plan their own campaigns.

The stages of planning are as follows:

1. RESEARCH

This takes many forms: economic research, market research, sales research, distribution research and promotional research.

There are two methods of carrying out this research: primary and secondary. Primary research is the gathering of information which is not normally available to the company commissioning the research. Most members of the public are familiar with this type of market research which is often carried out by interviewers using questionnaires with members of the public, or questionnaires which are completed by the customer. Interviews can be conducted in the street or over the telephone. Examples of this type of research in leisure and tourism would include interviews with 'frequent flyers' about airline or airport services, or a health club questionnaire about facilities given to customers to send by post after a visit. Some surveys are carried out by official bodies gathering information about trends in public spending and use of leisure time.

Secondary research (also called desk research) involves the use of information already available to a company. It may have been gathered for a different purpose – such as sales records – but could be used to obtain information specific to the promotion research. There are other sources of information readily available such as government statistics, other surveys which have been published (for example *Social Trends*), press cuttings, information from organisations such as Chambers of Commerce, Trade Associations etc. It is always preferable to start research by using this information first, as it is more economical and easily accessible.

The market is separated into *segments* which include: occupations, age groups, level of income, education. The type of promotion chosen must appeal to the types of customer segment targeted.

Analysis of this research will enable the company to identify its target market segment, the types of promotion which are likely to be successful and the costs involved.

ECONOMIC RESEARCH	MARKET RESEARCH	SALES RESEARCH	DISTRIBUTION RESEARCH	PROMOTIONAL RESEARCH
Investigating the local economy: high or low level of employment; investigating the national economy; bank rates, exchange rates	Identifying: potential customers and gaps in market; likely demand or decline in customer interest; competition; level of current customer satisfaction	Identifying trends and patterns in purchasing; success of current sales methods; evaluations of sales staff performance	Identifying points of distribution for leaflets, brochures: agencies, tourist attractions, libraries etc	Identifying appropriate types of advertisement or promotion for a particular product; the effectiveness of different promotional methods

TABLE 19 *Types of research*

ACTIVITY

Look at the dossier of leaflets and advertisements you gathered earlier (page 87), and separate them into the market segments you think they match, selected from: existing customers, new customers, age, gender, location, financial status, mobility, ability/disability, group, individuals. Ⓒ

2. PLANNING THE CAMPAIGN

In order to plan a campaign certain decisions have to be made:

a. What is the purpose (objective) of the campaign?

Is it to launch a new product or service, or to relaunch a product? Is it to raise funds? Is it to increase or win support?

Profit-making organisations will probably want to achieve the successful launch or re-launch of a product or service whereas voluntary or non-profit making organisations may want to raise money for charity or increase their membership or usage of facilities.

b. Who is the campaign aimed at?

One of the first steps in a promotional campaign is to identify the target for the campaign. It may be directly aimed at the customer, or it may be aimed at an intermediary, such as a wholesaler or retailer. In leisure and tourism the intermediary could be a travel agent or the management of a sports or leisure club. The target may be existing or potential customers.

It is important to identify the appropriate type of promotion to match the target audience and the type of product. For instance, advertising very expensive villa holidays in a cheap tabloid newspaper is unlikely to gain many customers.

c. What is the current situation?

With an existing product or service it is advisable to carry out a SWOT (strengths, weak-

Strengths	Weaknesses
Established reputation	Expensive
Well-known for reliability and service	Inadequate staffing levels
Convenience of location	No parking nearby
New attractive premises	Strong local competition
Opportunities	**Threats**
Original product	Introduction of minimum wage will increase staff wages
Employ experienced staff	
Offer of joint promotions with tourist board	Discount vouchers in newspapers for competing products
Access to cheap rate air tickets	
Selling via Internet	Closure of large factory nearby possible

SWOT analysis for a tour operator

ness, opportunities, threats) analysis. This will help to focus the campaign.

The above SWOT analysis was carried out by a specialist tour operator wanting to promote holidays through a regional office. By carrying out this analysis, they would be able to form their marketing plan. It may be necessary to examine the competitor's products more thoroughly, investigate the availability of experienced staff in the area or consider recruiting recently qualified students from a nearby college to improve staffing levels.

ACTIVITY

Draw up a SWOT analysis for a leisure and tourism facility known to you. Prepare a short report (ideally using a word processor) making recommendations based on the analysis. C N IT

3. SETTING OBJECTIVES

The next stage is to set objectives:

Once the objective (or objectives) is decided, the company or organisation must decide how it is going to achieve the objective. It may mean that there will be a short-term and long-term plan.

Short-term plans could be for:

- disposing of unsold seats for a theatre performance towards the end of a run;
- clearing stocks of sports equipment at the end of season;
- taking advantage of an offer made to the company (last-minute cheap holidays, ferry tickets etc).

Often, decisions will have to be made quickly for these types of promotion and the simplest way is to advertise the offers in newspapers and on commercial radio. Increasing use is also being made of the Internet and Ceefax for late offers for holidays.

Financial	Social	Community	Raising awareness	Attracting new customers	Changing an image
increase sales; increase profits; dispose of unsold products; take advantage of special offers	attract young people	increase usage of facilities; provide a meeting place for the elderly	increase knowledge of sport; announce opening of facility	encourage more members; regain custom lost to competitors	update to modern image; widen appeal to all age groups

TABLE 20 *Examples of objectives*

Longer-term plans (sometimes called strategies or long-term objectives) could be to:

- increase market share and profit (for instance by opening more outlets, taking over the competition's position as market leader);
- improve customers' awareness of the products on offer, for example by emphasising that something has been improved in some way (more departure points for holidays, longer opening hours of a swimming pool);
- co-operate with a complementary supplier; or
- participate in a relevant event (e.g. link with a watersports equipment manufacturer to produce a joint video filmed in a resort featured in your brochure);
- launch a new brand or product at a trade show or exhibition.

These objectives will be prepared as a 'brief' for the marketing consultant.

4. BUDGET

Included in the brief will be a budget set for the promotion, that is the amount of money allocated for it.

Costs to be considered in a budget include those for:

- Research
- Design and printing of promotional materials (brochures, point of sale, advertisements)
- Free gifts, vouchers for money off
- Advertising
- Distribution
- Staffing
- Demonstrations, visits, exhibitions

5. TIMING

The next stage will be agreeing the timing of the promotion. Many factors have to be considered when agreeing timing:

- Preparation (research, design and manufacturing of promotional items; visits to select venues for promotional activities, booking venues, advertisement slots on television, advertising space in press)
- Filming of a commercial or video presentation
- Administration of campaign (checking legal formalities, handling coupon returns)

- Training of promotion staff
- Distribution of materials (brochures, leaflets, point-of-sale materials)
- Setting up sales systems

External factors such as weather, competing activities and season will also have to be considered. Certain promotional activities follow a set pattern according to the type of business and whether the activity has to coincide with a specific trade show or event. New cars are traditionally unveiled at the Motor Show, held in the autumn; holiday shows are held during the winter period and brochures are released 6–12 months before the start date in the brochure, holiday advertising on television tends to be most concentrated over the Christmas period, and so on.

Timing is crucial in the release of holiday brochures. The largest operators have to work on very narrow profit margins and have to decide who will be the first to release a new season's brochure. The first one released will offer competitors an oppor-

Source: Pagis Scanwork, MGI, Software Corp.

tunity to undercut prices, and so this is quite a gamble. In recent years, operators have brought out more than one edition to enable them to adjust prices when they see what the competition is offering.

If you look at the timetable on page 92, you will see how far ahead a tour operator has to plan for the launch of a new product.

You will see from this timetable just how far ahead the tour operator would have to plan for the printing and distribution of the brochures, sending press releases to trade and

 ## CASE STUDY

Some years ago, a very large tour operator carried out a very successful campaign prior to the distribution of its latest brochure. Everything had gone according to plan, venues were booked for travel agents' launch parties, television advertisements had been giving previews of the new brochure and the date for first bookings to be taken, the sales team had been strengthened to increase representation in all the regions of the UK, and the brochures had been printed in Germany,

where printing costs were lower. The only factor that could not be planned was the weather, and that was when the plan fell apart. There was heavy fog for the whole week that the brochures were to be flown into the UK, and consequently the delivery was late, making distribution to travel agents a week later than planned, causing a great deal of frustration to travel agents and the public who were anxious to book holidays.

YEAR 1	Summer		First stages of research. Look at economic factors influencing the future development of package tours. Identify likely selection of destinations.
	September/ December	**RESEARCH/PLANNING**	Second stages of research. In-depth comparison of alternative destinations.
YEAR 2	January/ February		Decide on capacity for each tour, duration and departure dates. Initial negotiation with printer, including dates for printing brochure.
	February/ March	**NEGOTIATION**	Negotiate with the airlines for charter flights.
	March/April		Negotiate with hotels, transfer services, optional excursion operators. Early artwork and text under development at design studio, with layout suggestions.
	April/May		Establish hotel prices and arrange for contract with hotels and airlines. Contract with transfer services, etc.
	July	**ADMINISTRATION**	Determine exchange rates. Estimate selling prices based on inflation, etc. Galley proofs from printer. Any necessary reservations staff recruited and trained.
	August		Final tour prices to printer. Brochures printed and reservations system established.
	September/ October	**MARKETING**	Brochure on market, distribution to agents. Initial agency sales promotion, including launch. First public media advertising, and trade publicity through press, etc.
YEAR 3	January/ March		Peak advertising and promotion to trade and public.
	February/ April		Recruitment and training of resort representatives, etc.
	May		First tour departures.

Typical tour operator timetable

Source: The Business of Tourism. *J. Christopher Holloway (1985)*

public media, arranging for launching the brochure to agents at special events, and setting up the sales systems to cope with the first bookings.

Once all the materials have been produced and the staff trained to sell the new product, it is important that distribution takes place and that the appropriate press releases are sent out to coincide with the distribution. A slip up in part of the process could have serious consequences for a campaign.

When planning a promotional event, such as a marathon, extra time is needed to allow for the public to enter and train. Participants may also want to obtain sponsorship and the venue may need additional time to prepare

Source: Pagis Scanworks, MGI, Software Corp.

for the event. Preparations for major events like the Grand Prix Motor Races take several years.

The most commonly used forms of promotional activity in leisure and tourism are:

- **advertising**
- audio-visual aids
- **brochures**
- catalogues
- company visits
- **competitions**
  (for customers and the trade)
- design (product and packaging)
- direct mail
- directories
- **educational visits**
- financial incentives
- **free gifts**
- **guarantees**
- incentive schemes
  (to trade and own sales team)

- **leaflets**
- **merchandising**
- off-premises displays
- **packaging**
- **point-of-sale displays**
- premiums
- PR (press and public relations)
- **price reductions** (and pricing strategy)
- **special offers** (price, etc.)
- telephone selling
- tent cards
  (hotels, restaurants, department stores)
- **vehicle livery**
- year books

The activities shown in **bold print** have been the most used.

Source: Douglas Foster, Mastering Marketing, *2nd edn (Macmillan, 1984)*

6. SELECTING PROMOTIONAL TECHNIQUES

As shown, there is a very wide range of promotional techniques possible for use.

 **ACTIVITY**

The list of activities shown on page 93 was prepared in 1984. Review this chapter and identify which techniques have become more popular and which have become less popular since then. Add other techniques that are used today. Ⓒ

Monitoring the success of a campaign

It is important to monitor the success of a promotional campaign and this can be carried out in many ways. The most obvious pointer to success would be a massive increase in sales following one advertisement. However, since most campaigns involve several different techniques (press advertising, TV commer-cials and publicity events) it is difficult to measure which was the most cost effective method used.

Many companies will trace the origin of an enquiry over the phone by asking the caller where they heard about the product or service being requested. Keeping a note of the replies will enable the marketing department to measure which advertisements were the most successful. Providing vouchers or coupons for return by the public is another way of monitoring results. Giving a code to be used when writing for information can also indicate which newspaper the customer has read.

The demand for additional brochures or leaflets, however, does not necessarily mean that the campaign has succeeded – there could be an unconnected reason for high demand, such as school projects! Holiday brochures featuring wild animals in safari parks are particularly popular with young school children.

Large organisations will use market research companies to carry out interviews by post, telephone or in person to assess the impact of their advertising.

PORTFOLIO TASK

Investigate a leisure or tourism organisation and present a report on:

✔ the products and/or services the organisation offers

✔ details of pricing for those products and services

✔ where the product or service is provided

✔ the promotional methods used by the organisation

✔ research methods used to identify target markets

✔ the target markets which you think have been targetted by the promotions

✔ an example of one item of promotional material aimed at a particular target market

In addition, you should produce an imaginative and appropriate high-quality promotional item for a target market which you identify.

You should include an analysis of the marketing activities of the organisation and suggest ways of evaluating the success of the promotional techniques and materials used by the organisation. Give your opinion on the success or otherwise of the promotional activities.

You should identify the sources of materials you have used, and use the technical language accurately and appropriately.

Completion of this Portfolio Task should enable you to gather partial evidence for the following **key skills**:

N2.1 Interpret information from 2 sources.
N2.2 Carry out calculations to do with handling statistics.
N2.3 Interpret the results of your calculations.
C2.2 Read and summarise information.
C2.3 Write 2 different types of document about straightforward subjects.
IT2.1 Search for and select information for 2 different purposes.
IT2.1 Search for and develop information (if a computer is used).
IT2.2 Explore and develop information (if a computer is used).
IT2.3 Present combined information for 2 different purposes (if a computer is used).

CHAPTER 5

The provision of customer service in leisure and tourism

Illustration of customer service situation

Source: © *Life File/Dave Thompson*

There is a great deal of emphasis nowadays on providing good customer service. Watch any television commercial for products such as cars, insurance, and holidays and you will realise that service is used as a major selling point in promotion campaigns.

Supermarkets, with a great deal of competition, devote nearly all of a commercial to the service they provide, for example to parents of young children, or when making refunds. Very rarely do they mention the actual products they sell, as all supermarkets sell similar products and they can only compete by making the regular essential chore of shopping more enjoyable through the provision of good customer service.

In leisure and tourism, the majority of customers do not need to use leisure facilities or take holidays at all. They choose where, when and how they will spend their free time, and the number of organisations competing for their custom is expanding rapidly.

Why is good customer service important?

Providing good customer service is essential if companies are to gain new customers and retain the loyalty of their existing customers. Employees need to provide such a service to both internal and external customers. Internal customers are other employees in the same or associated organisation. For example, when a hotel receptionist passes messages to a housekeeper, the housekeeper becomes the receptionist's customer. Similarly, a travel agent requesting help from an airline would also become an internal customer of the airline.

External customers are essential to any organisation as without them, there would simply be no business.

What is customer service?

There are different types of customer services: those which are expected and those which are provided to enhance the customer's experience of a facility. Some aspects of service will be taken for granted.

For example, when booking a holiday, a customer expects a travel agency to provide:

- information
- booking arrangements
- payment facilities

However, since there are many travel agencies in all towns and cities, and most of them are selling exactly the same types of holidays, counter staff offering detailed resort information (possibly based on personal experience), a quick, efficient booking service, and a wide range of brochures to choose from, will gain more customers, will be recommended to friends and most importantly – gain repeat business.

Additional characteristics such as a tidy, well maintained agency, pleasant, well-groomed staff, comfortable browsing areas and free coffee, enhance the whole experience of booking a holiday.

The most important of all these characteristics is the quality of service provided by the staff. Knowledgeable staff, with good customer handling skills, can often compensate for small, cramped offices.

Similarly, a visitor to a sports centre will expect:

- a clean changing area
- appropriate equipment, e.g. in the gym
- basic health, safety and security requirements to be met
- trained staff

However, in order to compete in this expanding sector of the industry, sports centres now offer many more facilities. Many have revised their image by being changed to leisure centres and they have widened the activities and services they provide. In a typical leisure centre with a pool, there are possibilities of lane swimming, aquafit classes, special clubs for mothers and toddlers, over 50s or women only, and even aquanatal classes for expectant mothers. Support services offered range from swimming tuition to childcare, catering facilities, licensed bars, beauty salons, saunas, and a fully-equipped gymnasium.

Many sports or leisure centres which were formerly owned and subsidised by the Local Authority are now run as independent companies and have to be more competitive with each other. The effect of independence has been that leisure centres now have an increased awareness of the need to give good customer care training to their employees.

ACTIVITY

List the essential types of basic customer service which a customer expects in:

- **a theatre**
- **on an aircraft**
- **in a hotel** C

Implementing customer service

First impressions count!

Customer service starts even before a customer visits a facility. The first contact may be by telephone or letter or, increasingly, by fax and e-mail. It is therefore essential that a thoroughly professional and courteous manner is used to communicate at all times.

When a visitor arrives at a facility, the provision of parking spaces nearby and an attractive clean and tidy entrance all give a good first impression. Staff should be dressed neatly and appropriately. For example: business dress for a hotel receptionist, shorts and clean shirt for a swimming pool attendant. Name badges should

be worn. Reception areas should be free of dirty coffee cups, and provide clean comfortable seating, perhaps supplied with some newspapers or magazines where customers sometimes have to wait.

It is not only the first impression, but the overall impression of a facility that is important to a customer. After all, companies are as anxious to look after existing customers as new ones, and there is a need for repeat business. An impression is gained in many ways and there are many different, but important, points to consider when assessing the customer service provided by an organisation:

1 **General maintenance**
- Property and equipment – is it clean, tidy and well maintained?
- Vehicles – are they clean, regularly serviced?
- Tools – are they stored safely and are they up-to-date?
- Clothes/uniforms – are they clean, tidy, relevant?
- Toilets – are they cleaned regularly with sufficient supplies of soap, toilet paper, etc?

2 **Information systems**
- Signposts – are there enough and are they easily spotted?
- Public announcements – are they clear enough, can everyone hear them?
- Telephone and fax facilities – are these readily available?
- Emergency procedures – are these easy to follow, are they demonstrated?

3 **Accessibility**
- Disabled – what arrangements are there to assist the disabled? Do they work?

- Elderly – what facilities or special arrangements exist?
- Families – how are they accommodated, are there changing rooms for babies?
- Parking – is there sufficient space, is it well lit?
- Public transport – is it nearby, how often does it operate?

4 Convenience of payment

Does the company accept:
- credit cards
- cheques
- debit cards
- cash
- e-mail payments?

5 Communication

- Telephone – are there quick response, 24 hour service, answer-phone facilities?
- Fax and e-mail – does the company have this facility?
- Mail – is all mail acknowledged quickly and matters dealt with efficiently?
- Freephone and freepost – is this facility offered?
- Suggestion boxes – are these provided for customers and staff?
- Helplines – does the company offer a free helpline service?

Staff should greet visitors immediately. Even if they are on the telephone, they can smile a welcome. They should never carry on personal conversations over the phone or with a colleague when a customer approaches or is within earshot.

The majority of leisure and tourism organisations now have a 'Customer Care Policy' and this will set out clear company procedures for dealing with customers, dress codes and greetings. By training staff to follow these procedures, the company can ensure that all customers receive the same level of service. However, care is needed to ensure that responses do not become too automatic, as for example, in the USA where 'Have a nice day!' is often used automatically without any real meaning.

 **ACTIVITY**

Find out from your colleagues whether they have to follow customer care policies in their part-time employment, or visit a local facility such as a hotel, restaurant, night club, or pub and find out if their policy is on display anywhere, or if staff obviously have been trained. C

Personal presentation is an essential part of any customer care policy. Clothing must always be clean and well pressed, with no missing buttons, stains etc. Shoes should be clean and polished. Hair and nails should be clean and well groomed and the highest standard of personal hygiene required. As many leisure and tourism employees often work in hot and enclosed spaces, this last requirement is extremely important!

Other aspects of personal presentation include the attitude and personal behaviour of staff. Good communication skills and a sincere liking for people are essential in a service industry. A customer needs to feel valued and respected and appropriate body language such as a welcoming smile is the same in any language! In an international business such as tourism, where there could be language problems, this becomes even more important.

ACTIVITY

Look at the illustrations below showing possible facial expressions of service industry personnel that you or your customers could meet. For each one write down:

a) the messages conveyed to you by these faces

b) allocate a score out of ten for each one's probable 'Customer Care' attitude.

1.   a)

      b)

2.   a)

      b)

3.   a)

      b)

4.   a)

      b)

5.   a)

      b)

Source: Primer for COTOP Level 1, ABTA National Training Board

The tone of voice used should also indicate that you are interested in the customer and his or her needs. A bored response will be quickly picked up by the customer, and reflect badly on the organisation. Even if you have to answer the same question a hundred times a day, you must always remember that each customer only asks it once, and your answer is new to them. Careful use of language is important when you are dealing with particular types of customers, for example using simple language with a child or foreigner, speaking slowly and clearly to someone with hearing difficulties. Do not forget to pause and allow the customer to respond or ask further questions.

When handling telephone calls, you should always speak clearly and take care with pronunciation of difficult words. You may need to spell out some words, and it is useful to know the phonetic alphabet used for this. Another point to remember is that a smile can be transmitted over the phone! Some companies even insist that staff stand when making business calls as it makes them sound more efficient, but this is a little extreme.

ACTIVITY

Experiment with a partner the tone you use when phoning. Practise speaking clearly as if you were dealing with a foreign caller, use the international alphabet and ... smile! Then make the call in a different tone/pitch/at a different speed. Compare your notes as listeners. **C**

LETTER	PHONETIC EQUIVALENT	PRONUNCIATION
A	ALPHA	al fah
B	BRAVO	brah voh
C	CHARLIE	char lee
D	DELTA	dell tah
E	ECHO	eck oh
F	FOXTROT	foks trot
G	GOLF	golf
H	HOTEL	hoh tel
I	INDIA	in dee ah
J	JULIETT	jew lee ett
K	KILO	key loh
L	LIMA	lee ma
M	MIKE	mike
N	NOVEMBER	no vem ber
O	OSCAR	oss cah
P	PAPA	pah pah
Q	QUEBEC	keh beck
R	ROMEO	roh me oh
S	SIERRA	see air rah
T	TANGO	tang go
U	UNIFORM	you nee form
V	VICTOR	vik tah
W	WHISKEY	wiss key
X	X RAY	ecks ray
Y	YANKEE	yang key
Z	ZULU	zoo loo

The phonetic alphabet

QUESTIONING TECHNIQUES

To find out customers' requirements you need to be able to develop a good questioning technique. Your first question on approaching a potential customer or being approached is likely to be 'Good morning, how may I help you?' This is called an 'open' question and requires a response from the customer. If however, you simply said 'do you need any help?' to a customer who was browsing, the likely response is 'No.' This is a 'closed' question and will usually get a negative reply, ending the conversation and possible sale. Open questions always need more than one word in reply.

 ACTIVITY

Write down as many closed questions as possible which could be used in a leisure or tourism facility. Use them to question your group and then change the questions to open ones. Note the difference between the two types of responses. (C) 💬

NON-VERBAL COMMUNICATION

Non-verbal communication or body language is very important. Positive body language includes:

- standing or sitting properly
- eye-to-eye contact
- paying close attention to the customer
- careful listening
- not smoking, eating or drinking whilst on duty
- clean, tidy appearance
- high standards of personal hygiene

- letting a customer know you have seen them, even if you are dealing with another customer or a phone call
- never showing your personal feelings, even if you are having a bad day

This last point shows a professional attitude, as customers should never be aware of any problems that you may be having. Staff should not indulge in personal chats in front of customers either. Customers must always feel that they are the most important person to you and your organisation.

ACTIVITY

Role-play different customer service situations and practise positive and negative body language. Ⓒ

TELEPHONE COMMUNICATION

The general points above are also relevant when answering the phone. Large organis-ations will often have a set greeting when answering the phone, and number of rings permitted before it is answered. All employees need to:

- have pencil and paper ready to write down messages;
- answer promptly and give the greeting;
- state the name of the organisation;
- use a clear, friendly tone;
- find out the caller's name early on in the conversation and use it at least once, especially towards the end of the call;
- repeat back any details when you take a message;
- check difficult words and spellings, asking the caller to spell them if necessary;
- keep reassuring callers who are holding on – never leave them indefinitely. If they are likely to have a long wait, ask if you can call them back;
- always allow the caller to ring off first in case they forget something;
- Smile!

SPEECH PATTERNS	BODY LANGUAGE PATTERNS
1. Loud and rapid means I'm angry or impatient	1. Leaning back or away signals disinterest or dislike
2. High and rapid means I don't believe what I'm saying	2. Fidgeting or glancing away signals boredom
3. Monotone means I'm bored and think my product is rubbish	3. Closed hand indicates aggression or impatience
4. Slurred and sloppy means I can't be bothered	4. Pointed finger is commanding and aggressive
5. Rapid robot repetition means I've said this a million times and can't be bothered if you understand or not	5. Slouching or leaning shows carelessness
	6. Hands in pockets shows sloppiness
	7. Poor grooming shows you don't care about yourself and thus won't care about me

TABLE 21 *Negative speech and body patterns*   *Source:* Who Cares Wins

When making a call you should have a clear idea of what you want to say and who you want to speak to, have any necessary information in front of you, adopt a businesslike, but friendly, tone, and be brief to keep the cost down.

ACTIVITY

Using the checklist below, take it in turns to observe a partner answering the telephone. After observing several calls, discuss the results of your observations, and how you could improve on these. Ⓒ

Checklist

Telephone Procedure:

Answering the Phone

☐ Answer within three rings

☐ Greet the caller appropriately

☐ Give your name if possible

☐ Give your job or department as appropriate

☐ Ask how you can help

Transferring a Call

☐ Ask if caller minds being transferred

☐ Explain why it is necessary to transfer

☐ Explain who you are transferring to

☐ Make sure someone is there to transfer to

☐ Tell person who is on the line

☐ Tell person the nature of the call

Putting Caller on Hold

☐ Ask customer if they may be put on hold

☐ Wait for a response

☐ Tell customer why it is necessary for them to hold

☐ Give them a time estimate for their hold

☐ Explain if there is a queuing system

☐ Come back to them within the time limit

☐ Ask if they would like to hold further

☐ Offer other options

Taking a Message

☐ Ask the caller's name before you say someone is not there

☐ Explain colleague's absence positively

☐ Explain when colleague might return

☐ Offer to help person yourself

☐ Offer to take a message

☐ Get all the relevant information

Ending the Call

☐ Confirm any action you have agreed on

☐ Double check any important information

☐ Offer any other help

☐ Thank the customer for calling

☐ Let caller hang up first

☐ Record any important information

Source: Who Cares Wins – *Charts and Checklists*

WRITTEN COMMUNICATIONS

Increased use of modern technology has reduced the amount of written correspondence in most organisations, but you may still be expected to write or respond to:

- letters requesting information, or to make bookings
- messages to pass on to other employees or customers
- signs to advise customers
- itineraries for travellers
- agendas for meetings
- booking documents for facilities, holidays, coaching

You will also be expected to create customer records such as

- membership details
- customers' preferences
- details of holidays booked
- sales records
- fitness charts

In addition you will probably be required to complete documentation relating to stock, sales, and health and safety issues.

It is extremely important that you always complete any written communication clearly, accurately and that you check it. You must also file such records in such a way that any other colleague can find them easily.

You should never betray confidential information to any one. You must be discreet at all times, especially when dealing with outside callers who may want information about a customer. Any information that is stored on a computer database is subject to the Data Protection Act, and should only be used for the purpose for which it was supplied.

Customer care policies

The Customer Care Policy will normally start with a 'Mission Statement' which declares the intention of the organisation to provide a good service.

> 'IT IS OUR AIM TO ACHIEVE A LEVEL OF SERVICE EXCELLENCE WHICH EXCEEDS CUSTOMER EXPECTATIONS'

Cocks Moor Woods Leisure Centre, Birmingham

This Leisure Centre has recognised the need to meet MORE than the customer expects.

The Mission Statement for the Premier House Group not only gives its aims as far as customers are concerned, it also emphasises the benefits to its employees of providing good customer service.

ACTIVITY

Investigate the provision of customer service of one leisure or sports centre, and one travel agency and list the types of service provided. Share the information you have gathered with other members of your group and discuss which organisation offers the best customer service for your age group. Take a note of any 'Mission Statements' and whether the staff appear to follow set procedures, wear name badges etc. If possible, ask if there is a written procedure for Customer Care, but ensure that a facility is only approached once for this information by your group. C

PREMIER HOUSE MISSION STATEMENT

'The Premier House aim is to be the provider of Food, Drink and Accommodation to the customer, representing a value for money proposition. In modern day terms it sets out to provide the services associated with the Traditional Inn.

Our intention in providing this offering is to appeal to a substantial and growing market: to achieve standards of quality and service which will ensure success and provide realistic return on capital employed.

We further intend to provide our employees with an environment which encourages their progress and development to achieve job satisfaction'.

In turn each House has the aim of:

OPERATIONAL AIMS

'We must be the first choice pub in our market catchment area because we as a team will all demonstrate:

- A passion for customer care that is second to none;
- An obsession with excellent standards and value for money;
- The dedication to making customer and employees matter everyday.

Achieving these targets will enable us to deliver the sales and profit growth which is for the benefit of customers and employees alike'.

Example of a mission statement

THE 'PLUS' FACTOR

Following that activity, you will probably realise that the company which you agree provides the best service is one which actually exceeds expectations.

Organisations are aware of this and many employees are trained in customer handling skills even though it is not immediately obvious that they will have direct customer contact. They all need to know appropriate ways of addressing customers and how to behave when approached by a customer. For instance, a street cleaner would not normally be considered as an employee handling customers, but Birmingham City Council has trained its staff to be able to assist visitors to the city if necessary. Some have even taken lessons in foreign languages.

The Council wanted to ensure that all visitors to the city received a warm welcome from public employees. This has obviously helped to increase the popularity of Birmingham as a major conference venue, most recently hosting the Eurovision Song Contest and the G8 Summit Meeting. Both these events were seen by up to 100 million viewers worldwide, and are proof of Birmingham's success since the City Council decided to develop and market the city for business tourism.

Customers rarely notice service when it meets their expectations, as shown in the examples for travel agencies and leisure centres. They will certainly notice poor service, but will be more likely to recommend an organisation which more than meets their expectations. The travel agent who anticipates that a customer may need something more than they requested, such as airport assistance for the elderly, or a child's meal on the aircraft, or a leisure centre assistant who volunteers additional services to a harassed mother such as the childcare crèche, are all exceeding expectations.

Good customer handling skills rely on the integrity of the individual employees and their interest in the well being of their customers. They must meet the needs of individual customers, and more. They must want customers to enjoy themselves and to gain the most from their visit.

CASE STUDY

Gardening is one of the major leisure activities in the UK and the increase in the number of garden centres has led to improved awareness of customer needs. Not only do centres now provide appropriately labelled plants, they offer free advice leaflets and drop in advice centres, talks to clubs and societies, large well-laid out parking areas for cars and coaches and catering and toilet facilities.

Webbs Garden Centre in Droitwich has won an award for the best garden centre in England for many years. It is attractively laid out with large car parks, a variety of trolleys and carts, excellently laid out sections for different types of plants, shrubs and trees, a children's safe play area, free advice, tours to famous gardens, an excellent gift shop, regular free offers sent out with a newsletter to all householders in the area, and even free car boot liners to carry plants home.

The high number of visitors to the centre has encouraged them to open up separate sections for garden pools, furniture, landscaping, conservatories and other garden buildings. Special events take place in the summer months. They have also started giving plant vouchers to customers to pass to local schools.

Providing all these additional services has increased the popularity of Webbs so much that it is now classed as a 'Tourist Attraction' by the Tourist Board, not just a garden centre. What used to be a simple visit to buy plants has now become a very different type of outing, suitable for all the family. Very few visitors leave without buying something, even if it is just an ice-cream.

Staff also need to be aware of 'internal customers' i.e. other colleagues or companies with whom they are in contact on a regular or infrequent basis. They should also understand the structure of the company, and different people's responsibilities, as well as basic health, safety and security regulations.

Leisure and tourism organisations depend on repeat business as well as new customers, and the only way to attract and retain customers is by providing good customer service. Obviously a hotel which can attract groups on a regular basis, has much more security because it is guaranteed a certain number of guests a year. This means that jobs are more secure – a point all employees should remember (refer back to the Premier House Mission Statement on page 106).

There are many opportunities for customers to spend their leisure time and money. A day out could include a visit to a theme park, the cinema, a tourist attraction or a sports match, all of which are freely available in most areas of the country. A family choosing a cinema outing will not only be interested in the film which is being shown but also:

- accessibility
- easy parking
- catering facilities
- prebooking arrangements

Garden centres are now offering a far wider range of services
Source: Webbs of Wychbold

 **ACTIVITY**

With a partner consider the problems faced by smaller cinemas and suggest ways in which they could compete with multi-screen complexes by providing good customer service. Discuss your ideas with the rest of your group. Ⓒ

The benefits of providing good customer service

Employees of organisations which provide good customer service benefit in several ways:

- increased job satisfaction and self-esteem
- job security, with long-term prospects
- pleasant working conditions

It is very difficult to be happy working in an organisation where customers are always complaining. Such companies usually have a very high staff turnover.

Organisations which provide good customer service benefit by:

- increased sales and profits
- low staff turnover
- stronger market share
- possibilities of expanding
- customers' recommendations
- improved public image

Disneyland Paris added new attractions

However, poor customer service can have a devastating effect on a company.

It has been estimated that a customer who has a bad experience with a company will tell about 17 people, whereas a satisfied customer will tell only four.

A company can change a dissatisfied customer into a satisfied one simply by the way it responds to a complaint. Sir Richard Branson, of Virgin Airlines, ensures that all complaints are handled seriously. Not only does he instruct his staff to telephone customers directly to discuss their cause for complaint, he also telephones customers himself. This personal contact makes a great deal of difference to winning back customer loyalty.

 # CASE STUDY

When a large American-style theme park opened in Europe a few years ago there were many complaints. Start up problems included the long queues and high prices and failure to appreciate the needs of European customers and the group's market.

The park was modelled on those in America and some customers resented this lack of sensitivity towards its European location. Coach parking and the facilities for coach drivers – who often have to wait around for many hours for their groups – were very poor, and some organisers refused to take any more groups there. The owners changed their strategy in several ways after a new sales team was appointed in 1993:

- by making a visit more affordable;
- by lowering food prices, and introducing seasonal rates;
- by introducing more rides and entertainment, to spread the visitors around the park more, thus shortening waiting times for rides;
- by changing the names of some of the rides to more European names (even though some of them were merely a direct translation from their American names);
- by appointing executives to deal with group organisers directly;
- by improving drivers' restrooms and coach parking.

By 1995 group sales had increased so much that they had to appoint three wholesalers to handle group business from the UK alone. The park was renamed and relaunched, and extra all-year facilities added, such as a cinema and evening entertainment complex. Special events are also organised throughout the year, such as a Bonfire Party and a Dancing Festival.

The special events combined with the off-season lowered prices increased visits to the park during the winter months. Coach visitors to the park from the UK increased by 50% between 1996 and 1997.

There is obviously a clear link between the increased visitor numbers and the changes made to the image of the Park and the additional facilities provided, as a result of listening to customers.

Delayed passengers are particularly difficult to satisfy, and airlines are often not responsible for the delays. However, Virgin Airlines have been known to offer free return flights for another holiday to be taken at any time for families delayed on their return home from an off-season holiday in the USA, which is an extremely generous offer, especially as Virgin is classed as an economy airline.

When purchasing holidays from a brochure, a customer is relying on the advice of the travel agent and the honesty of the descriptions given by the tour operator, and they are unable to try the holiday venue out beforehand. This has often led to discontented holidaymakers, whose only compensation is perhaps a part-refund on their return from holiday. To remove any doubts, Thomson Holidays introduced a 'Money-back' Guarantee as shown on page 112.

Handling complaints

Most companies will have a complaints procedure. It is important that you know how to handle complaints. Although, unfortunately there are a few 'professional' complainers, such as people who deliberately look for faults in order to get their money back after a holiday, most people do not like to complain. The British in particular are very reluctant to complain about bad service. It is quite common to overhear customers in a restaurant moan about the food and then when asked by the waiter if everything is to their satisfaction they will say 'Fine thanks'! However, they usually do not go back to that restaurant.

When you do receive a complaint you should:

- *listen* carefully
- try to calm the customer down if necessary
- if possible, take them away from the main customer service area to talk to them

- always acknowledge written complaints promptly, and promising to deal with the matter
- *apologise* for the fact that they have felt the need to complain, but *without agreeing* they have cause to complain. This is very important as there may be legal implications.
- *promise* to investigate and *do so*
- *inform* the customer of the results of your investigation and make amends. This could be by offering to change something like a hotel room, make a refund, offer a free meal, ticket, voucher against services
- if your suggestion is not acceptable, ask the customer what he would like done and improve on his suggestion if you can
- agree on a course of action
- make sure that action is carried out
- keep the customer informed during the investigation
- complete all relevant paperwork to register complaints and *ensure that this will not happen again*
- follow up with a letter or phone call.

Most importantly, you must take responsibility for helping the customer to solve the difficulty.

 ACTIVITY

Use the following complaints form for completion during role play with your group on various situations related to potential complaints regarding leisure and tourism services. When you have completed the records, write out suggestions for making amends to the customer. Write a letter, using a word processor, to one of the complainants making an offer of compensation. Ⓒ ⒤⒯

Date

Time

Member of Staff

Department

Customer Name

Address

Phone No.

Specific Nature of Complaint:

Proof of Purchase?

Date of Purchase?

Action Taken

Do you think Customer was satisfied by your action?

Does this complaint signal a Widespread problem?

Does this complaint indicate a serious design, delivery or quality fault?

Should we as a company be looking for a larger problem which this complaint might indicate?

Signature

Supervisor

Sample complaints form

Guaranteeing customer service

Source: Thomson Holidays Ltd.

Your holiday rights

From booking a holiday to arriving in the resort, many things can go wrong. We explain what you're entitled to if you're let down

Booking the holiday

Before you book, read the brochure and booking conditions carefully. Brochure descriptions form part of your contract and you can claim compensation for any loss you suffer because of misleading or inaccurate descriptions. Also read the description of your accommodation in the *OAG Agents' Gazetteer* –ask your travel agent to show you a copy.

Check with the tour operator to find out if there are likely to be any disturbances from building work near your hotel. If you have a particular requirement (wheelchair access, say) agree this before booking and ensure that it's noted on your invoice.

Tour operators must protect your money so that you don't lose out if they cease trading. Our advice is to book only with tour operators or travel agents that hold a government-approved bond, such as those organised by the Association of British Travel Agents (ABTA), the Federation of Tour Operators (FTO), the Association of Independent Tour Operators (AITO) and the Association of Bonded Travel Organisers Trust (ABTOT).

When booking charter flights, or a package holiday which includes flights, always use a company with an Air Travel Organisers' Licence (ATOL) and get valid airline tickets or an ATOL receipt with the name/licence number of the ATOL holder.

If plans get changed

Your tour operator must inform you if it makes significant changes to your holiday. Before you agree to any changes, check whether the booking conditions allow the operator to make the proposed changes and find out as much as you can about the new arrangements.

If you decide to go ahead, write accepting the changes under protest and reserve your rights to claim compensation later. If you don't accept the new plans, you are entitled to take an alternative package or claim a refund and maybe compensation too.

Tour operators usually try to limit their liability in such cases by stipulating maximum compensation amounts in their booking conditions. However, holidaymakers have often succeeded in winning more, by arguing in court that these limitations are unfair.

In the resort

If you arrive at the resort to find your hotel is overbooked or any other important element of your holiday isn't provided, the tour operator must make alternative arrangements. If this isn't possible or you have grounds to refuse the alternative, you're entitled to be brought home.

The tour operator is responsible for all parts of the package, even where they are provided by contractors (like the hotel owners, say), so report any difficulties to the tour operator's representative in the resort. The rep should either rectify the problems or move you to alternative accommodation.

If things are not put right, gather evidence of the problems (photographs, video footage, and copies of complaint forms) and swap names and addresses with any holidaymakers who have the same problems. If you accept compensation on the spot, make it clear you're doing so under protest, and don't sign anything that would prevent you from claiming more later.

Flight delays

When an airline fails to get you to your destination within a reasonable time of the scheduled arrival, you may be entitled to compensation. But you'll need to prove that the airline could have prevented the delay. For flights which are part of a package, you should complain to the tour operator. Travel insurance might provide compensation for very long delays.

Luggage

Make sure your luggage is labelled with your name and destination, and include your home address inside the case. If your luggage doesn't appear at your destination or is damaged when it arrives, fill in a Property Irregularity Report at the airport.

Airlines are liable for losses resulting from delay, and loss or damage to luggage, but compensation is limited to around £15 a kilo. If your luggage is more valuable than this, you should make a 'declaration of interest in delivery' when you check in. This will entitle you to higher compensation for delay or loss. You may be able to claim for lost luggage on your travel insurance instead, though some policies exclude damage incurred while luggage is in the care of the airline.

On your return

If you want to complain, write to the tour operator's head office, asking for compensation for loss of value, loss of enjoyment and out-of-pocket expenses. Be persistent even if your initial request is refused. If you're not satisfied with the response, you can use the ABTA arbitration scheme, or take your case to the small claims court.

For claims higher than the small claims court limit of £5,000, another option is to club together with other holidaymakers who suffered the same problem, and share the costs of a court action. Group actions are an increasingly popular and successful way to seek redress.

Source: Which?, *July 1999*

It is important that you always treat every complaint – however frivolous it sounds to you – as serious. You must also know when something is too serious for you to handle and who you need to contact about it. Most customers would have no objection to being told that you have referred the matter to your supervisor.

DISCUSSION

Discuss any complaints you have had to make to organisations with the rest of your group. How were these complaints handled? Were you offered a replacement, refund or something else? Were you happy with the outcome? Would you use this organisation again?

Types of customers

Leisure and tourism customers cover every type of human being, but can be classified as:

- individuals
- groups
- people of different ages
- people from different cultures
- non-English speakers
- people with specific needs
- businessmen and women

They all have needs in common:

- courteous, honest treatment
- efficient pre-sales service
- the opportunity to buy goods and services easily
- efficient after-sales service
- helpful, fair complaints procedures
- fair and honest pricing
- health, safety and security procedures

Customers generally are now educated to expect high standards of service. Programmes such as 'Watchdog' and organisations such as the Consumers' Association have increased their awareness of their rights as consumers. Consumer protection laws with regard to sell-

INDIVIDUALS	GROUPS	DIFFERENT AGES	DIFFERENT CULTURES	NON-ENGLISH SPEAKERS	SPECIFIC NEEDS	BUSINESS
Single rooms Privacy Billing arrangements Extra security	Special check-in Group leader contact Discounts Special meal times	Entertainment Childrens clubs Nursery Teenage discos Discounts Senior citizen facilities Cots	Religious considerations Special diets Respect for different customs	Interpreters Translations Graphic explanations, such as maps, signs, pictures	Access Hearing loops Guide dog facilities Braille menus Assistance with wheelchairs Adapted premises Special diets Taped commentaries	Speedy check-in and check out Itemised billing Special lounge Conference facilities Telecommunications

TABLE 22 *Categories of customers and their needs*

ing goods and services have also increased the public's awareness of their rights. However, most leisure and tourism customers want to purchase a service or goods, not complain.

Each of the groups identified earlier have slightly differing additional needs:

INDIVIDUALS

These could be independent travellers, young mothers attending a keep-fit class on their own, or a group of individuals brought together through a common interest, as for example on a package holiday. These customers can easily be overlooked, especially if there are other more demanding groups present. It is important not to overlook the needs of the individual and treat them just as well as anyone else. Unfortunately it is still very common for single travellers to be given the worst room in a hotel, near the lift shaft, overlooking a back yard, over the kitchen etc., in spite of the fact that many single rooms are more expensive. Individual diners are often placed in the worst position in a restaurant. Single people are often more vulnerable than groups when travelling or staying in a hotel. It is therefore very important, for example, that hotel staff ensure that they are discreet when issuing keys. They should not call out the room number for anyone nearby to hear. Good hotels now train their staff to be aware of this, and some even provide rooms on 'ladies only' floors. Companies which specialise in holidays for single people have recognised their needs by offering them seats at a table together with other 'singles', and added security features.

GROUPS

When handling groups it is essential to identify a group leader and if possible to channel all communication through the leader only. It may be necessary to arrange special facilities such as booking in, handling luggage, mealtimes, early calls, coach parking and so on. Group organisers expect to be treated well, as they know their custom is important and there is always the possibility of repeat bookings. A group organiser would probably be given a good room in the hotel and is often given additional incentives to return such as gifts, vouchers, free wine with meals and so on.

Groups are offered better prices for each group member and often additional benefits, such as: separate entrances, prior boarding or check in facilities, separate dining areas or travel packs. Groups that travel regularly together are likely to receive promotional offers, such as advance bookings, publicity material for use in their usual meeting place to advertise visits, and events, such as cruise evenings or wine tastings (paid for by a travel agent, cruise company, tour operator or tourist attraction).

PEOPLE OF DIFFERENT AGES

This could include families, school and student groups, senior citizens groups, all of whom have different requirements.

SPECIAL REQUIREMENTS

Customers may have many types of special requirements. The most obvious need is assistance for people with physical or mental impairments. Recent changes in the law have led to improved arrangements for people with mobility problems. Specially adapted entrances, lifts, toilets and car parking areas are becoming more available, but there is still room for improvement. Larger organisations have made the most progress in this respect,

ACTIVITY

Study the following advertisement for GNER. Identify the benefits offered to groups and also the customer service facilities provided for all passengers. Refer to the earlier check lists. Ⓒ

Within the advertisement:

GNER

High Performance
Luxury Group Travel

Just Look at the benefits

- Fast journey times
- Direct to the heart of major towns and cities.
- Complimentary seat reservations.
- Groups seated together.
- Luggage assistance arranged
- Refreshments can be arranged in advance.
- Quoted prices are guaranteed
- One ticket covers your whole group.

The Great North Eastern Railway Group Travel Service can take you to and from London Kings Cross, Peterborough, Leeds, York, Newcastle, Edinburgh and Glasgow.

If a group of 10 or more are making a trip for business, social or educational purposes, we'll make sure your trip with Great North Eastern Railway is rewarding. We take you to the heart of major towns and cities quickly and in comfort. A group of 10 or more is eligible for a 10% group discount in First class accommodation, or 25% in Standard, subject to availability. The more flexible you are, the greater the discount and you can choose from a wide range of trains for an extremely competitive price.

We can accommodate special business needs, catering for all, ranging from three-course meals, light snacks or just a refreshing drink - there is a selection of drinks and snacks to suit everyone.

Other benefits from this service include complimentary seat reservations, situated together, and luggage assistance. Quoted prices are guaranteed and one ticket covers the whole group.

Lines are open from Monday to Friday 09.30 - 16.30, with an out of hours answerphone service. Simply leave your message and we will return your call. Alternatively write to or fax us at the address below.

Source: Group Travel Organiser magazine

Access is the biggest problem for carers with small children and often prevents them from using facilities. Approach paths and footways should be wide enough for a double pushchair/wheelchair to pass (1.8m). Footways should be flat and level with covers and gratings not more than 20mm wide, non-slip and laid flush with footway service.

SIGNS, ADVERTISING BOARDS

Signs to be pole or wall mounted avoiding sharp and jagged edges, with overhanging objects to be at least 2.5m above footway.

ENTRY TO LEISURE CENTRE

Ideally access should not involve a change of level, but where unavoidable there should be ramps at least 1.8m wide at all entrances constructed of a material with good surface grip. Where gradient is steeper than 1:20, provide steps.

CAR PARKING

Sufficient parking spaces and to include clearly marked wider spaces of 3.2m in addition to disabled parking bays, for users with pushchairs.

BARRIERS

It is essential to have external barriers between entrances and roads or entrances and car parks.

THRESHOLD

Small children are likely to trip over raised thresholds so these should be flush. Doormats to be inset flush with floor level to prevent tripping and slipping.

SINGLE DOORS

Doors need to have an opened width of 900mm to give access for a double pushchair or wheelchair. The clear wall space to the side of an opening door must be at least 300mm for ease of movement. Doors should not be heavy to open and should be designed to stay open at 90 degrees.

DOUBLE DOORS

Double swing doors are preferable in circulation areas, designed to be pushed open by a pushchair and not too heavy. Clearance of 2.5m between two sets of double swing doors. One door to have a minimum width of 800mm to allow independent access by wheelchair users and single pushchairs.

GLASS IN DOORS

Safety glass (toughened or laminated) always to be used in doors which should be clearly marked at child and adult heights to prevent people walking into them. Visibility panels positioned at child and adult heights are important so that children behind doors can be seen. Glass not lower than 400mm above floor finish.

HANDRAILS: DOOR HANDLES

Handrails at child height (610mm) and adult height (840mm) should be provided on staircases and door handles at a maximum 1m above floor level, for children's use. Level door handles that return are preferable to knob handles.

REVOLVING DOOR/TURNSTILES/ AUTOMATIC DOORS

Revolving doors and turnstiles are difficult and dangerous for children and their carers. Revolving doors deny access to wheelchair users and an alternative side-hinged door should be provided. Automatic doors are preferred by many carers with small children but the following precautions must be taken: vertical lasers at a range of levels and low enough to read a child who has fallen in the path of the doors; weight sensors that respond to child weight.

PUSHCHAIR PARKS

A covered lockable outside space, or space just inside the entrance to the leisure centre, should be designed for prams and pushchairs. Alternatively, coin-operated lockers, or lockable rail, or cloakroom facility for storage.

STAIRCASES

Ramps and lifts should be provided wherever possible. Where stairs are used the following should be noted. Open risers to be avoided as children can slip through. Risers no higher than 170mm and uniform. Treads not less than 250mm deep. Staircases at least 120mm wide to allow adult and child to ascend/descend holding hands. Handrails both at child and adult height on both sides of the staircase.

FEEDING AND BABY CHANGING FACILITIES

Purpose-designed facilities should be available so that babies and toddlers can be fed in comfortable, hygienic and dignified circumstances. Feeding and changing are two different activities that are not suitably combined, and should be available equally to male and female carers.

FEEDING AREA

Carers are likely to have other children, bags or pushchairs with them, so it is important to allow a generous space (a minimum of 7.5sq m is recommended for one carer with two children). Privacy for breast feeding mothers should be provided. The feeding area should provide comfortable seating with low cushioned arm rests; facilities for heating milk/food; low/high feeding chairs with safety harnesses; playpen, play equipment or wall-mounted activity board for accompanying child; sink for rinsing bottles, cups etc.

NAPPY CHANGING AREA

Bench measurements to be 1.5m long × 600mm wide × 800mm high per baby to provide adequate space for baby and placing bag, nappy etc. A fold-down shorter bench is possible but must be designed so there is no danger of collapse. Easy-clean surfaces and enclosure on three sides is preferable, with a raised lip to prevent babies rolling off. Disposable paper towel roll, a nappy dispensing system and nappy disposable unit; sink or sluice with lever taps.

CHILDREN'S TOILETS

Child-sized toilets 305–355mm high should be provided, and washing and drying facilities are needed at both adult and child heights. Child-sized pedestals or wall mounted wash basins to be between 450–550mm high.

Child access guidelines

Source: Leisure Management, *Vol. 9 No. 3 1987*

CONTENTS

Contents of a booklet aiming to improve tourism accessibility
Source: Tourism For All booklet, published in association with Glaxo Holdings p.l.c. and the National Tourist Boards of England, Scotland, Wales and Northern Ireland

with some restaurant chains providing such facilities as Braille menus, staff who can use Sign Language for the deaf, facilities for guide dogs. Carers accompanying anyone with an impairment should be accommodated. Some organisations offer free entrance to carers and reduced entrance fees for anyone unable to partake fully of any activities because they are impaired. An obvious example of this would be a theme park, as many rides would be unsuitable.

Safety precautions are extremely important for all ages, but in particular, children need to have:

- secure surroundings, for instance in a crèche or nursery, with a booking in and out system
- appropriate sleeping and eating arrangements
- safe equipment in play areas and pools
- professional supervision when using equipment
- traffic conditions to be regulated, for instance 5 mph in hotel grounds.

When dealing with the elderly it is important to remember that they are not all necessarily frail, and could be quite upset if you suggest that they are! However, with tact it is possible to find out if they need any assistance, for example with carrying luggage, or climbing into transport. You should remember that generally they:

- feel the cold more than young people
- have smaller appetites
- use toilet facilities more frequently
- can tire easily
- cannot walk long distances

- may not be able to climb stairs
- react more slowly
- may have difficulty carrying things
- are sometimes forgetful, which makes them frustrated.

Special arrangements are necessary for people with physical or mental impairments. You can obtain further specialised information related to this from RADAR and other organisations, which give precise details regarding size of access doors to enable wheelchair access, etc.

PEOPLE FROM DIFFERENT CULTURES

It is extremely important that you respect different cultures. In an international business like leisure and tourism, you will meet many nationalities and this can be very rewarding, but you must remember that just because they do something differently to you, you should accommodate them. Our eating habits seem strange to other people too!

You need to remember that:

- they may be used to a different alphabet, e.g. Greek, Chinese, Japanese, Arabic;
- they may be offended very easily by different aspects of body language – touching, for instance is forbidden between unknown males and females in some cultures. It is useful to find out what your visitors find offensive, if you regularly have visitors from a certain country. You could obtain help from the Chamber of Commerce on this or the Embassy;
- eating times and habits may be very different. You should always check on these requirements;

CASE STUDY

International airports can be busy confusing places, even for experienced travellers. Most travellers are likely to be slightly stressed, and are probably tired, especially if they have arrived on a long haul flight or are in transit. They may be experiencing jet-lag, and their 'body clocks' could be confused, with regard to eating and sleeping times. For this reason it is extremely important that every effort is made to smooth the traveller's way through an airport. If you do not speak the language of the country, it can be even more stressful. British Airways show a video in different languages, prior to arriving at Heathrow Airport, to explain the procedures on landing for passport control and transit to other terminals. International signposting for common needs, such as information, refreshments and toilet facilities are very helpful. British Airways also print a section in their '*High Life*' in-flight magazine to help new arrivals.

Source: High Life, *November 1999*

- graphic signs and sketch maps can be very helpful;
- broadcast messages in English will not be of any help to them.

You should keep lists of embassy numbers and interpreters if you have a regular need to help overseas visitors. There is a Language Link service available in emergency, and the police can give you this number.

The main requirement is at all times to be friendly, patient and tolerant. Put yourself in their place and think how you would feel.

ACTIVITY

Visit a local hotel or transport terminal and note down the facilities for:

- **children**
- **the elderly**
- **the mentally or physically impaired**
- **overseas visitors.**

Legal requirements

All customers expect organisations to abide by the law and there are many aspects of British Law which affect the leisure and tourism industry. An employee would be expected to be familiar with the general principles behind the laws in order to safeguard themselves, the public and their employer. The main types of laws affecting leisure and tourism are:

- Public liability
- Consumer protection legislation
- Health, Safety and Security

1. PUBLIC LIABILITY

Under the Public Liability Act all premises with public access must be insured against any incident that may arise as a result of an accident or other occurrence. The notice of insurance must be displayed on the premises.

2. CONSUMER LEGISLATION

These are laws to protect the customer and the main Acts affecting leisure and tourism are:

- Trades Description Act 1968
- Supply of Goods and Services Act 1982
- Consumer Protection Act 1987
- Consumer Credit Act 1974
- Misrepresentation Act 1967
- Race Relations Act 1976

The Trades Description Act is particularly relevant to any service business because the customer usually cannot try the service out before purchase, as they could with a product. The travel industry, in particular, has to be extremely careful to abide by this Act, as an agent is merely selling a 'holiday'. This can mean different things to different customers and it is not always easy to guess what a customer really has in mind. It is extremely important that the agent and the customer read resort and accommodation descriptions very carefully to ensure that the right choice has been made. If people seeking a quiet restful holiday are sent to a hotel in the middle of the disco district, they will have good reason to complain when they return if the agent has not pointed this out before they booked. The agent has to sell on the information given in the brochure, plus their own personal knowledge of a resort or information gathered from a neutral source such as an Agent's Gazeteer. Under the Trades Description Act, verbal and written descriptions of resorts have to be truthful and tour operators must check all the facts before printing their brochures.

3. HEALTH, SAFETY AND SECURITY

Everyone has a responsibility for their own health, safety and security, whether they are customers or employees. This responsibility has been reinforced by various Health, Safety and Security Acts that have been introduced over the years. The most well-known of these Acts is the Health and Safety at Work Act.

In addition to this Act, there are others which affect leisure and tourism, relating to conditions at work, the safe use of equipment, storage and use of dangerous chemicals, loading and unloading of goods and use of equipment such as protective clothing and electrical products.

Employees in the leisure and tourism industry need to know the basic requirements of these Acts and how they apply to them. For instance, you should always take action if you spot a potential hazard at work, such as a slippery floor or faulty electrical equipment. All employers should provide procedures to follow in the case of accidents and emergencies.

 CASE STUDY

A young couple wanted to book a holiday with their daughter aged 18 months in the Canary Isles in November. The enquiry was made over the phone to a well-known travel agent and their only requirements were: somewhere warm by the beach, with a supervised crèche. The travel agent promised to investigate likely resorts, and came back with one which she said 'is exactly what you need – it's got lovely self-catering bungalows, there's a crèche and children's play area and it's on the beach'.

As the agency had run out of winter brochures, the agent showed the wife the summer brochure, which did indeed include what they wanted, with a crèche, so she

booked it. However, when the couple arrived in the resort, they were extremely distressed to find out that there was no crèche in November, and this was clear in the winter brochure. Therefore, they would not be able to spend any time alone without their daughter. This was the couple's first holiday since she was born and they were really looking forward to spending their mornings swimming and diving together without having to worry about her. Their whole holiday was ruined simply because the agent did not check that the facilities were available all year round. Had the agent checked the winter brochure, the situation could have been avoided.

CASE STUDY

The following report on water slide safety was published by the consumer 'watchdog' magazine, *Which?*

Water slide safety

We inspected ten water slides and found safety problems with them all

Just how safe are water slides? They are an increasingly common feature of swimming pools and water parks. But, according to the Sports Council and the Health & Safety Commission (HSC), they are also a frequent source of minor injuries. Some people have even drowned as a result of using them.

We sent a water safety expert to take a detailed look at the special water facilities (including slides) at ten sites around the UK, and found that none followed all the appropriate safety guidelines. The main findings for each of the sites are shown opposite. Some of the failings relate specifically to the design or operation of the water slides; others relate to general pool safety. But all are important to ensure the safest possible use of water slides and other facilities.

CHUTES AND FLUMES

There are more than 200 swimming pools or water parks with slides in the UK. Sometimes water slides are called flumes, hydro-slides or chutes. The vast majority are in pools owned by local councils, but some are in privately-owned leisure centres or holiday camps.

Most slides are permanent and range in length from about 30 to 100 metres. They are often in the form of tubes which snake round, and many pools have more than one slide. In most cases, you simply slide down them on a stream of water, although on some you have to lie on a mat, or sit on a ring or raft.

SAFETY GUIDELINES

There are three main codes of practice covering the design and operation of water slides in the UK. These have been issued by the Sports Council and the HSC (as part of their guidance on pool safety), the Safety in Leisure Research Unit, and

the Institute of Baths and Recreation Management. All three are voluntary, so pools and parks don't have to follow them, and the fact that there are three is unnecessarily confusing. We think it would be clearer and safer if there was a single set of rules which all water slides had to follow.

INADEQUATE SUPERVISION

One of the main dangers we found was inadequate supervision of slides and pool areas. More than half the pools we visited had a notice at the entrance saying that parents were responsible for the behaviour of their children on the slide. It's true that parents shouldn't just rely on the lifeguards. But this doesn't mean that pool operators can get away with unsatisfactory supervision by their staff. We found too many cases where lifeguards who were supposed to be controlling the slides didn't enforce their own safety rules.

Sometimes there just weren't enough guards on duty; sometimes those who were on duty were standing in the wrong places — some tried to control slides only from the bottom, for example. This breaches the safety guidelines from the Sports Council and the HSC, and is potentially dangerous. There should always be a lifeguard at the top of the slide as well as one at the bottom.

BUILDING PROBLEMS

Some of the biggest problems with water slides are due to bad design. There isn't even a British Standard for water slide design, although a European standard is now being developed.

Pool safety guidelines from the Sports Council and the HSC say that clear markings to show how deep the water is are 'particularly important.' But half of the pools visited by our safety expert had not complied with even this simple guideline.

KNOCKED UNCONSCIOUS

Pool B was badly lit, while the Pool C had coloured tiles. These are also against pool safety recommendations. It's important for lifeguards to be able to see the bottom of pools easily: some pool deaths reported in the last few years have been as a result of incidents where children were knocked unconscious and drowned because nobody saw them lying at the bottom of the pool in time.

Five out of ten pools didn't have guard rails around dangerous parts of the pool. These are necessary to stop people falling in, or to remove the temptation for children to dive or jump in. One was particularly hazardous, because it had an inadequately guarded routeway close to very deep water.

All three codes of practice state that pools should provide clear signs, which set out how each slide should be used. But none of the sites we visited met this standard. Too much of the advice was incomprehensible or confusing. For example, one safety leaflet was clear and well designed, but it contradicted the advice given on posters about rider position and age rules. This leaflet has now been withdrawn.

VERDICT

Safety has to be the top priority for water slide operators. We're worried by the number of safety failings our inspector found. It is often seemingly small details which cause serious accidents on water slides. Operators need to pay more attention to the safety guidelines so that everyone can have a great time on water slides, secure in the knowledge that each slide is as safe as possible. Having fun on a slide and being safe aren't — or shouldn't be — incompatible.

Source: Which?, *March 1993*

Duties of employers

It is the duty of every employer to safeguard, so far as is reasonably practicable, the health, safety and welfare of all those in his or her employment. This duty is extended to others who may be affected by the operation of the facility, e.g. contractors, visitors and members of the general public. In practice the employer must have specific regard for the following:

1 To provide plant and equipment that is not a risk to health.
2 To ensure that work systems and practices are safe.
3 To ensure that the work environment is regularly monitored in respect of health and safety requirements.
4 To provide safe storage for substances that could pose a threat to safety and ensure their safe use.
5 To provide a written statement of safety policy and bring it to the notice of employees (applies only to those employing five or more staff).
6 To provide adequate information and training for all staff in matters relating to health and safety.

Duties of employees

Employees have a duty under the HSW Act to:

- Take reasonable care to avoid injury to themselves or to others by their work activities.
- To co-operate with their employers and other agencies to ensure that the requirements of the Act are carried out.
- Not to interfere with or misuse anything provided to protect their health, safety and welfare under the Act.

Source: GNVQ Leisure and Tourism, *Ray Youell,*
Pitman Publishing (1994)

 ACTIVITY

1. **Visit a local leisure centre or swimming pool. Make a list of any potential hazards at the centre and prepare a report similar to the one from *Which?* on page 123, using a word processor.** (C) (IT)

2. **Referring to your own part-time employment or perhaps a visit to a tourist attraction, obtain information on the training employees receive regarding health and safety procedures.** (C)

Security is another important aspect for leisure and tourism customers. Any facility that is used by children has to be particularly careful about vetting employees' history and also ensure that the area is secure against intruders or children wandering away. Adult customers need to feel that they and their belongings are safe. This is achieved by:

- providing key cards, safes, door chains and spy holes in hotels
- secure record-keeping for checking in and checking out children
- locking up files holding customer records
- providing locked changing rooms and lockers in leisure centres
- never disclosing information about customers to third parties.

TP's tips for survival

- Stay alert and anticipate problems, such as dimly lit areas, shady looking characters, the hotel bar romeo.
- Never open a hotel door before establishing who is outside. If in doubt, call the hotel management.
- Avoid badly lit areas of hotel car parks – if necessary, drive to the entrance and get a member of staff to park the car for you.
- Use women-only carriages on trains if available.
- Do not wear expensive jewellery or watches that could be snatched on the street.
- Carry a credit card holder with expired or supermarket plastic – a mugger is not likely to inspect the contents before legging it.
- Pack a small wedge for jamming under hotel doors.
- Take care not to wear clothing that might cause offence in some countries.
- Ensure someone knows your movements – fax the office or inform hotel reception.
- Wear something in bed at night if alone in a hotel – all sorts of people have access to your room.

Source: TP Direct Magazine

Employees also need to be aware of their own safety and security at all times, especially when handling large sums of money or taking it to a bank, or working late at night. Additional legislation covers such matters as licensing premises to provide alcohol and entertainment, fire regulations related to venues and events, street collections, running lotteries and food hygiene regulations.

ACTIVITY

1. **Research different Acts relevant to leisure and tourism in the library or over the Internet.** **C** **IT**

Case Study: Safety in Jamaica

Concern about the safety of visitors to Jamaica has, for several years, caused the Foreign and Commonwealth Office (FCO) to issue advice about muggings, drugs and other crime, no-go areas, and public transport. Only one agent in ten saw fit to tell us this.

THE QUESTION

We told the agents that we wanted a romantic holiday for a couple. The customer's partner had concerns about safety on the island. What advice could the agent give?

THE RIGHT ANSWER:

The FCO advice warns visitors:

- to be alert for thieves
- to exercise caution when walking in isolated areas, even in daylight
- not to resist in the event of a robbery
- not to walk alone on beaches, or at night

- to avoid areas of Kingston and be careful when travelling between airport and resort
- to avoid public transport unless ordered from the hotel.

Agents who fail to pass on the FCO advice or to communicate its contents are, in our view, negligent. A Spanish court recently found a travel agent liable for damages together with the tour operator, after the death of a child in a violent incident in Egypt. The agent had failed to pass on information regarding civil unrest.

WHAT THE AGENTS SAID:

Shamefully, almost 40 per cent of agents either gave no safety advice at all or assured us that the destination was safe. Many agents obviously felt that the fact that a tour operator operated a programme to a destination somehow guaranteed its safety.

The best answer
One in 10 agents (24) used their computer or the trade publication ABTA Magazine to access the FCO advice, then either read it out, allowed the inspector to read it, and/or handed over a copy of the advice. Lunn Poly performed best of the chains, with just under a quarter of its agents passing on the FCO advice. Over half of the Going Places branches gave no advice or asserted that Jamaica is safe.

The worst answer
Frankly, there are too many to enumerate. We confess to total puzzlement over the Winchester agent who checked the FCO advice on computer and then solemnly declared: 'No, there's nothing on there for Jamaica – so no problems at present!' And we almost admire the sang-froid of the Cardiff agent who sang the praises of the place, despite her own experience of being held up at machete point and robbed on the beach! A number of agents blithely assured us that there were no warnings in place, but made no attempt to verify that this was the case, saying, for instance, that when there are warnings they flash up on the screen, but neglecting to put this to the test.

Our advice
As it would appear that agents cannot be trusted to volunteer safety information, we'd suggest that you specifically ask whether there is any FCO advice on your intended destination. The agent can call it up on screen while you are there. Keep a note of what you are told. You may have a claim against the agent if the position has been misrepresented to you.
You can check things out for yourself on the Internet at www.fco.gov.uk

Source: Extract from Which?, *Report on Travel Agents, 1999, (Consumers' Association).*

FINANCIAL RECORDS	EMPLOYMENT RECORDS	CUSTOMER RECORDS
Income	Staff records	Orders
Outgoings	Pay records	Reservations (travel, hotel rooms)
Tax and VAT	Sales performances	Payments
Profit and loss		Subscriptions
Bank statements		Bookings (theatre seats,
Invoices		coaching, facilities)

TABLE 23 *Record-keeping in business*

Keeping customer records

Although many records in leisure and tourism are now held on computers, it is often still necessary to create handwritten or typed record cards and files. Accurate and up-to-date records help to ensure the smooth running of an organisation. There are many types of records kept in a business (see Table 23).

Confidentiality and security of information

It is essential that all customer records are handled in a confidential manner. Staff should never pass information on to third parties, however persuasive an enquirer may be. This is especially important when dealing with VIPs or celebrities and where there is likely to be a security threat, as in, for example, the case of a politician likely to be a target for terrorist action. In particular, hotel staff have to be very discreet about the guests in a hotel, and never reveal who is staying there to outsiders. The Press is particularly persistent in trying to find out this type of information.

All customer records should be kept in a secure place, and confidential information on computers should only be accessible to essential members of staff, using passwords for access. Discs should be stored in a locked fireproof container, and ideally backed up on other discs. Any information recorded on computers is subject to the Data Protection Act.

Obviously the large organisations such as hotel and travel agency chains, tour operators and leisure attraction operators are likely to have completely computerised systems. Hotels, for example, often have a direct link from the bar till to guest invoicing and stock control, so that when a guest orders a drink it is automatically invoiced to him on his room bill and the replacement is ordered to top up stocks. However, many smaller organisations still rely on handwritten or typed records: for example, small tour operators, local museums, and theatres.

HOTEL AND GUEST HOUSES	TRAVEL AGENTS, AIRLINES, TOUR OPERATORS	LEISURE CENTRES AND SPORTS FACILITIES	TOURIST ATTRACTIONS, MUSEUMS, THEATRES
Reservation charts	Initial enquiry forms	Membership application and subscription records	Membership and subscription records
Registration forms	Booking records		
Key release forms	Copies of vouchers issued	Fitness programmes	Individual and group bookings
Luggage and safety deposit receipts		Booking charts for courts, classes, coaching	Tickets issued
Arrival and departure lists	Booking confirmations		Booking confirmations
	Invoices		
Travel agents' vouchers	Monthly booking returns	Score cards	Invoices
Restaurant and bar bills	Tickets issued	Competition charts	Mailing lists
Extras bills	Receipts	Equipment records	
Guest history cards	Reservation charts		
Group booking forms and rooming lists			
Invoices			

TABLE 24 *Types of customer records*

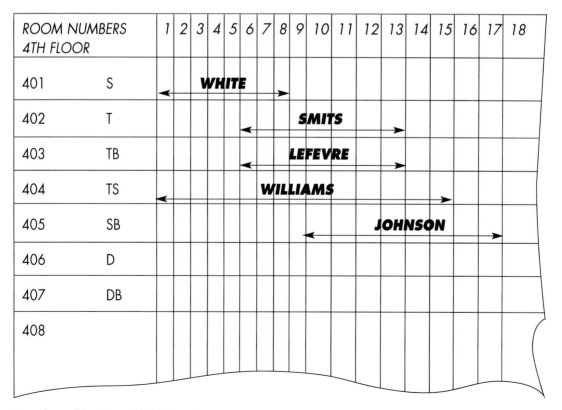

Part of a small hotel's monthly booking chart

```
          LEISURE COMPANY LEISURE CENTRE

Application No ........  New Membership No ......

               MEMBERSHIP APPLICATION

*I/We apply for *FAMILY/ADULT/JUNIOR/SENIOR CITIZEN
MEMBERSHIP

SURNAME................................*MR/MRS/MS

FIRST NAMES                      DATE OF BIRTH

1 ...............................   ..............

2 ...............................   ..............

3 ...............................   ..............

4 ...............................   ..............

ADDRESS: ......................
                                 2 passport
.............................     photos per
                                 person required
.............................

TELEPHONE NUMBER MUST BE GIVEN

TEL NO. HOME: .............. WORK ..............

*Delete as appropriate

Cheque/PO to be made payable to:
Leisure Company plc
----------------------------------------------------
I agree to abide by the rules of the centre

Date ................  Signature ...............

The centre reserves the right to refuse membership.
----------------------------------------------------
FOR OFFICE USE ONLY

Date received ........  Fee received ............

Receipt No        Cheque/PO No
----------------------------------------------------
Membership fees: adult  £45.00   junior £20.00
                 family £100.00  senior citizen £20.00
```

An example of an application form for membership of a leisure centre

It is important that records are completed promptly, as soon as possible after a transaction. For example, immediately a hotel receives a booking for a room, that needs to be entered on the reservations chart, so that the room does not get double booked.

Manual charts are often completed by using symbols or colour codes to demonstrate the stage of the booking: enquiry, provisional or confirmed. Any amendments made to records must always be complete, accurate and up to date.

This type of chart could also be used by a small tour operator offering private villas, or to book a facility, for example a tennis court.

ACTIVITY

1. **Prepare a weekly chart, suitable for manual completion, for use by a small leisure centre offering: four tennis courts, a small learner swimming pool, 4 squash courts, 2 sunbeds and a 2-person sauna.**

2. **Look up the terms of the Data Protection Act and summarise them for an employee in a leisure centre or health club.** Ⓒ

PORTFOLIO TASK

1. You will need to research one leisure or tourism organisation and prepare a report about the customer service. The report should include:

✔ **a description of the organisation or facility and the services it offers;**

✔ **a description of the customer service situations and the ways in which the organisation meets the needs of different internal and external customers, with specific examples matching all types of customer;**

✔ **a contrast between the different ways that internal and external customer situations are handled;**

✔ **the customer complaints procedures;**

✔ **the types of customers records kept, with examples;**

✔ **an evaluation of the customer service that is provided;**

✔ **an explanation of why good customer service is important to the organisation;**

✔ **an analysis of the consequences of poor customer service for the organisation.**

2. You should be observed in a customer service situation, and demonstrate your own ability to:

✓ handle customers in a variety of situations, including the handling of complaints;

✓ communicate effectively and confidently, and handle customers in a friendly positive manner, providing them with valid information and assistance;

✓ complete at least three different types of customer records (manual, computerised and for different types of leisure and tourism services);

✓ evaluate your own performance.

Completion of this Portfolio Task should enable you to gather partial evidence for the following **key skills**:

C2.1a Contribute to a discussion (with customers).

C2.2 Read and summarise information.

C2.3 Write 2 different types of document about straightforward subjects.

IT2.1 Search for and select information for 2 different purposes.

IT2.1 Search for and develop information (if a computer is used).

IT2.2 Explore and develop information (if a computer is used).

IT2.3 Present combined information for 2 different purposes (if a computer is used).

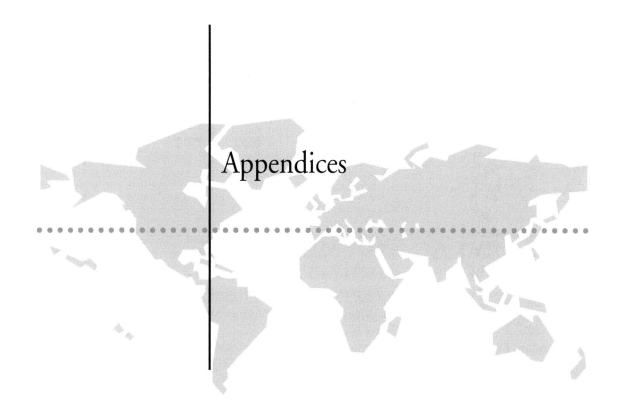

Appendices

Appendix 1

EMPLOYMENT IN TOURISM RELATED INDUSTRIES (JUNE 1990 AND JUNE 1998)

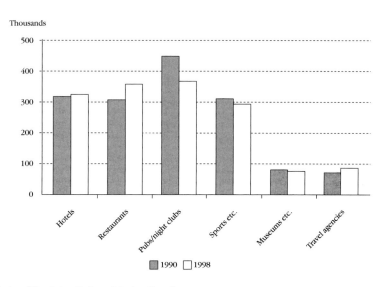

Source: Office for National Statistics, Labour Market Trends

Note: Refer to Table 25 for detailed definitions of bars on x axis (see Appendix Two)

Appendix 2

EMPLOYMENT IN TOURISM RELATED INDUSTRIES IN GREAT BRITAIN

EMPLOYEES IN EMPLOYMENT	STANDARD INDUSTRIAL CLASSIFICATION	JUNE 1990 '000	JUNE 1995 '000	JUNE 1997 '000	JUNE 1998 '000	CHANGE JUNE 98/97 %
Hotels and Other tourist Accommodation	551/552	314.4	331.5	327.3	318.7	−2.6
Restaurants, cafes and snack bars	553	303.0	332.7	344.4	356.0	+3.4
Public houses, bars night clubs and licensed clubs	554	445.8	393.1	376.5	364.1	−3.3
Travel agencies/ Tour operators	633	70.0	82.1	82.1	83.5	+1.7
Libraries, museums and other cultural activities	925	80.0	77.5	73.7	77.0	+4.5
Sports and other recreational activities	926/927	311.5	319.7	298.3	291.7	−0.7
Total		1,524.7	1,536.6	1,502.3	1,491.1	−1.3

TABLE 25 *This table indicates the number of employees in tourism related industries in Great Britain since 1990.*

Source: Labour Market Trends, Office for National Statistics

Comments:

(a) In June 1998 there were an estimated 1,491,00 employees (excluding the self-employed) in tourism related industries in Great Britain. Compared with June 1997 employment in the above tourism related sectors had fallen by 11,200 or by 1.3%. Hotel and catering industry lost 8,600 but restaurants and cafes gained some 11,600 jobs. It is interesting to note that 62% of jobs in the above SIC categories are taken by women and nearly three quarters of part-time jobs are also taken by women. (December 1997 estimates). Since 1990 travel agents and tour operators have created 13,500 new jobs but the industry lost some 33,600 jobs between June 1990 and June 1998.

(b) Employment in the above SIC group plus self-employed accounted for 6.2% of all the employed labour force which was 27,041,000 in December 1997.

(c) According to the Office for National Statistics there were 194,000 self-employed people in tourism related industries in Great Britain in 1997. This is an approximate indication of the self-employed in the tourism industry.

(d) It is estimated that, for every one direct job in the tourist industry, half of an indirect job is created elsewhere in the economy.

Appendix 3

TYPES OF TELEVISION[1] PROGRAMME WATCHED: BY AGE (1997)

UNITED KINGDOM								PERCENTAGES
	4–15	16–24	25–34	35–44	45–54	55–64	65 AND OVER	ALL AGED 4 AND OVER
Drama	24	29	27	26	26	25	24	25
Light entertainment	17	18	17	16	15	14	15	16
News	9	10	12	14	16	18	19	15
Documentaries and features	10	13	15	15	15	16	14	14
Films	10	14	14	14	14	13	11	13
Sport	6	8	7	8	8	8	10	8
Children's programmes	23	5	6	3	2	2	2	5
Other	2	3	3	3	3	4	5	3
All programmes	100	100	100	100	100	100	100	100

[1] Data are for terrestrial channels only.

TABLE 26

Source: Broadcasters' Audience Research Board: British Broadcasting Corporation: RSMB Ltd; Taylor Nelson Sofres Ltd.

Appendix 4

DEPARTMENTS OF MEDIA, CULTURE AND SPORT

THE ARTS	MUSEUMS AND GALLERIES	HERITAGE	INTERNATIONAL	LIBRARIES
Arts Policy	British Museum	English Heritage	European Union cultural relations	British Library
The Arts Council	National Gallery	Royal Commission on the Historic Monuments of England	Council of Europe cultural relations	Local authority libraries
Crafts Council	Victoria and Albert Museum	National Heritage Memorial Fund	Export licences for works of art etc	Office of Registrar of Public Lending Rights
Broadcasting, media and films	Natural History Museum	World Heritage Convention	**Sport and Recreation**	**Other departments for Culture Media and Sport functions**
Broadcasting, film and media policy	National Museum of Science and Industry	Royal Estates	Sport and recreation policy in England	Information including national statistics
The BBC	Tate Gallery	Historic Royal Palaces Agency	Sports Council for England	(particularly broadcasting and tourism)
Independent Television Commission	National Portrait Gallery	Historic Royal Parks Agency	Safety of Sports Ground legislation	Citizen's Charter within the Department's area of responsibility
The Radio Authority	Imperial War Museum	**National Lottery**		
Channel 4	National Maritime Museum	Lottery policy		
S4C Channel 4 Wales	National Museums and Galleries on Merseyside	OFLOT		
British Film Institute	Royal Armouries, Leeds			
British Film Commission	Tower of London			
Press regulation	Funding certain trustee museums			
Tourism	Museums and Galleries Commission			
Tourism policy	Works of Art and other Cultural Objects of National Importance			
British Tourist Authority				
English Tourist Board				

TABLE 27

Appendix 5

PARTICIPATION[1] IN HOME-BASED
LEISURE ACTIVITIES: BY GENDER

GREAT BRITAIN					PERCENTAGES
1996-97	1977	1980	1986	1990-91	
Males					
Watching TV	97	97	98	99	99
Visiting/entertaining friends or relations	89	90	92	95	95
Listening to radio	87	88	87	91	90
Listening to records/tapes/CDs	64	66	69	78	79
Reading books	52	52	52	56	58
DIY	51	53	54	58	58
Gardening	49	49	47	52	52
Dressmaking/needlework/knitting	2	2	3	3	3
Females					
Watching TV	97	98	98	99	99
Visiting/entertaining friends or relations	93	93	95	97	97
Listening to radio	87	88	85	87	87
Listening to records/tapes/CDs	60	62	65	74	77
Reading books	57	61	64	68	71
DIY	22	23	27	29	30
Gardening	35	38	39	44	45
Dressmaking/needlework/knitting	51	51	48	41	37

[1] Percentage of those aged 16 and over participating in each activity in the four weeks before interview.

TABLE 28

Source: General Household Survey, Office for National Statistics

Appendix 6

VALUE OF TOURISM AND CONSUMER SPENDING IN THE UK 1977–1997

The table below compares tourism spending with total consumer spending in the UK economy. All tourism spending represents just over 6% of all consumer spending (10.5% if day visitors spending of £21.0 billion (1996) is included). This proportion reached its lowest level in 1982 at 5%, but since then has fluctuated between 5.2% and 6.0% in 1997. It must be noted that since 1989 the basis for collecting domestic tourism has been changed.

| YEAR | INTERNATIONAL TOURISM | | | DOMESTIC TOURISM | | | |
	OVERSEAS £M	FARES £M	TOTAL £M	DOMESTIC £M	ALL TOURISM SPEND £M	ALL CONSUMER SPEND £M	TOURISM AS PROPORTION OF CONSUMER SPEND %
1977	2,352	624	2,976	2,625	5,601	86,887	6.4
1978	2,507	653	3,160	3,100	6,260	100,219	6.2
1979	2,797	745	3,542	3,800	7,342	118,652	6.2
1980	2,961	792	3,753	4,550	8,303	137,896	6.0
1981	2,970	788	3,758	4,600	8,358	155,412	5.4
1982	3,188	849	4,037	4,500	8,537	170,650	5.0
1983	4,003	1,020	5,023	5,350	10,373	187,028	5.5
1984	4,614	1,210	5,824	5,975 #	11,799	200,261	5.9
1985	5,442	1,375	6,817	6,325	13,142	218,947	6.0
1986	5,553	1,310	6,863	7,150	14,013	241,554	5.8
1987	6,260	1,480	7,740	6,775	14,515	265,290	5.5
1988	6,184	1,500	7,684	1,850	15,534	299,449	5.2
1989	6,945	1,750	8,695	10,875 ##	19,570	327,363	6.0
1990	7,748	2,025	9,773	10,460	20,233	347,527	5.8
1991	7,386	1,800	9,186	10,470	19,656	365,469	5.4
1992	7,891	2,100	9,991	10,655	20,656	383,490	5.4
1993	9,487	2,375	11,862	12,430	24,292	406,569	6.0
1994	9,786	2,550	12,336	13,220	25,556	427,394	6.0
1995	11,763	2,825	14,588	12,775	27,363	446,169	6.1
1996	12,290	3,080	15,370	13,895	29,265	473,845	6.2
1997P	12,244	3,050	15,294	15,075	30,369	506,130	6.0

New basis from 1984 onwards ## New survey

TABLE 29

Sources: Travel Trends and Economic Trends, Office for National Statistics
UKT Survey, ETB and the National Tourist Boards

Appendix 7
ADDITIONAL READING LIST

1. Books
Dictionary of Travel, Tourism and Hospitality, S. Medlik, Heinemann.
The Development and Management of Visitor Attractions, J. Swarbrooke, Heinemann.
From Tourist Attractions to Heritage Tourism, P. Yale, Elm Publications.
Quality in the Leisure Industry, Longman.
Leisure Participation: Free Time in the Global Village, Cushman, Veal and Zuzanek, CAB International.
Leisure and Tourism Services, N. Borett, Macmillan.
Recreation and Leisure, an introductory handbook, Venture Publishing.
Urban Tourism, C. Law.
Urban Tourism: Attracting Visitors to Large Cities, Mansell.
Core Geography: Leisure, F. Martin and A. Whittle, Hutchinson.
The Leisure Environment, M. Colquhoun, Pitman Publishing.
Marketing for Tourism, J.C. Holloway and R.V. Plant, Pitman Publishing.
Travel Geography, R. Burton, Pitman Publishing.
Business of Tourism, J.C. Holloway, Pitman Publishing.
Travel Industry Law, J. Downes and T. Paton, Pitman Publishing.
Travel and Tourism, P. Lavery, Elm Publications.
Successful Tourism Marketing, S. Briggs, Kogan Page.
Grand Tours and Cooks Tours, L. Withey, Auram Press.
Chandlers Travels, J. Carter, Quiller Press.
Effective Advertising and P.R., A. Corke, Pan.
Cooks Tours, E. Swinglehurst, Blandford Press.
Smooth ride guides (for the disabled travellers), FT Publishing.

2. Trade journals

Leisure Management, Portmill House, Portmill Lane, Hitchin, Hertfordshire SG5 1DG.

Travel Trade Gazette, City Reach, 5 Greenwich View Place, Mill Harbour, London E14 9NN.

Travel Weekly, Reed Business Information, Oakfield House, Perrymount Road, Haywards Heath RH1 3DH.

Group Travel Organiser Magazine, Landor Travel Publications, 250 Kennington Lane, London SE11 5RD.

Group Leisure Magazine, Yandell Publishing Ltd., 9 Vermont Place, Tongwell, Milton Keynes MK15 8BR.

Appendix 8

SOME USEFUL WEBSITE LINKS

Note: This list is not comprehensive and new sites are being added daily, but they should help you with your research and will also guide you towards other sites.

The Department for Culture, Media and Sport:
http//www.culture.gov.uk/TOURISM
The Department for Education and Science:
http//www.dfee.gov.uk
The Department of Transport, Environment and the Regions (DETR):
http//www.detr.gov.uk
Qualifications and Curriculum Authority:
http//www.qca.org.uk
Further Education Development Associaton GNVQ Support:
http//www.feda.ac.uk/GNVQSupport
CCTA Government Information Service:
http//www.open.gov.uk/
Sport England:
http//www.english.sports.gov.uk
SPRITO (National training organisation for sport, recreation and allied occupations):
http//www.sprito.org.uk/
Institute of Leisure and Amenity Managers (ILAM):
http//www.ilam.co.uk
Institute of Sport and Recreation Managers (ISRM):
http//www.isrm.co.uk
The Sports Industries Federation (SIF):
http//sportslife.org.uk
Institute of Sports Sponsorship (ISS) – Sportsmatch:
http//www.sportsmatch.co.uk
Business in Sport and Leisure (BISL):
http//www.bisl.org
United Kingdom Sports Institute (UKSI):
http//www.english.sports.gov.uk/uksi.htmBritish
Olympic Association (BOA):
http//www.olympics.org.uk
Manchester Commonwealth Games:
http//www.manchesteronline.co.uk/2002
Sports Aid:
http//www.sportsaid.orag.uk

The Football Association 2006 World Cup Bid:
http//www.fa2006.org
Football Licensing Authority FLA:
http//www.flaweb.org.uk
The Football League:
http//www.football-league.co.uk
Star UK (UK Tourism research liaison group):
http//www.staruk.org.uk
Guardian newspaper:
http//www.GuardianUnlimited
Source News (on Arts, Leisure and Recreation):
http//www.sddt.com/files/librarywire
The Ramblers Association:
http//www.ramblers.org.uk
Country Lanes bicycle tourism business:
http//www.countrylanes.co.uk
The lottery:
http//www.lottery.merseyworld.com
Lottery Sports Fund:
http//english.sports.gov.uk/lottery
Rollerworld:
http//www.rollerworld.co.uk
Lords Cricket Ground:
http//www.lords.uk
UNESCO (World Heritage Sites):
http//www.unesco.org
Office for National Statistics:
http//www.ons.gov.uk
British Tourism Authority:
http//www.visitbritain.com
English Tourist Board:
http//www.travelengland.org.uk
Scottish Tourist Board:
http//www.scotourist.org.uk/stb/
Wales Tourist Board:
http//www.tourism.wales.gov.uk
Northern Ireland Tourist Board:
http//www.interknowledge.com/northern-ireland/index.htm
Yorkshire Tourist Board:
http//www.digital-yorkshire.co.uk

Essex Tourism:
http//www.essex.gov.uk
London Tourist Board:
http//www.LondonTown.com
West Country Tourist Board:
http//www/dcs/ex/ac/uk/wcol/html
South East England Tourist Board:
http//www.seetb.org.uk
North West Tourist Board:
http//www.nwtb.u.net.com
English Nature:
http//www.english-nature.org.uk
Heritage Motor Museum:
http//www.stratford.co.uk
Ironbridge Museum:
http//www.vtel.co.uk
Royal Doulton Visitor Centre:
http//www.royal-doulton.com
Wedgwood Visitor Centre:
http//www.wedgwood.co.uk
Spode Visitor Centre:
http//www.spode.co.uk
Bass Museum:
http//www.bass-museum.com
Destination Sheffield:
http//www.sheffield.city.co.uk
Royal Armouries Museum:
http//www.armouries.org.uk
Natural History Museum:
http//www.nhm.ac.uk
Royal Observatory, Greenwich:
http//www.nmm.ac.uk
National Trust:
http//www.nationaltrust.org.uk
Theme and Leisure Parks Guide:
http//www.themeandleisure.com
The Tourism Society:
http//www.toursoc.org.uk

Appendix 9

TOURISM CONTACTS IN ENGLAND

English Tourism Council
Thames Tower
Black's Road
Hammersmith
London W6 9EL
Website: englishtourism.org.uk

Regional Tourist Boards:

1   Cumbria Tourist Board
    Ashleigh
    Holly Road
    Windermere
    Cumbria LA23 2AQ

2   East of England Tourist Board
    Toppesfield Hall
    Hadleigh
    Suffolk IP7 5DN

3   Heart of England Tourist Board
    Woodside
    Larkhill Road
    Worcester
    Worcestershire WR5 2EZ

4   London Tourist Board
    Glen House
    Stag Place
    London SW1E 5LT

5   Northumbria Tourist Board
    Aykley Heads
    Durham DH1 5UX

6   North West Tourist Board
    Swan House
    Swan Meadow Road
    Wigan Pier
    Wigan
    Lancashire WN3 5BB

7   South East England Tourist Board
    The Old Brew House
    Warwick Park
    Tunbridge Wells
    Kent TN2 5TU

8   Southern Tourist Board
    40 Chamberlayne Road
    Eastleigh
    Hampshire SO5 5JH

9   West Country Tourist Board
    St. David's Hill
    Exeter
    Devon EX4 4SY

10 Yorkshire Tourist Board
    312 Tadcaster Road
    York YO2 2HF

11 British Tourist Authority
    Thames Tower
    Black's Road
    Hammersmith
    London W6 9EL

12 Department for Culture, Media & Sport
    2–4 Cockspur Street
    London SW1Y 5DH

Source: Extracted from A Framework for Action, *published by English Tourism Council*

Appendix 10

WORLD HERITAGE SITES IN THE UK

1986   The Giant's Causeway and Causeway Coast

1986   Durham Castle and Cathedral

1986   Ironbridge Gorge

1986   Studley Royal Park, including the ruins of Fountains Abbey

1986   Stonehenge, Avebury and associated sites

1986   The Castles and Town Walls of King Edward in Gwynedd

1986   St. Kilda

1987   Blenheim Palace

1987   City of Bath

1987   Hadrian's Wall

1987   Palace of Westminster, Abbey of Westminster, and St. Margaret's Church

1988   Henderson Island

1988   The Tower of London

1988   Canterbury Cathedral, St. Augustine's Abbey, and St. Martin's Church

1995   Old and New Towns of Edinburgh

1995   Gough Island Wildlife Reserve

1997   Maritime Greenwich

Source: World Heritage Sites – UNESCO

INDEX

Page numbers in *italics* refer to charts and diagrams.